# PRAISE FOR WALT HARRINGTON

"A compelling and important book . . . It's been a long time since I have read anything as moving, and inspiring, as the passages about the relationship between Harrington and his father."
— *The Washington Post* on *The Everlasting Stream*

"This beautifully written book is about life's true values . . . Read it and count your blessings."
— President George H. W. Bush on *The Everlasting Stream*

"A message in a bottle floated out to white America about black America's remarkable diversity and resilience."
— *New York Newsday* on *Crossings*

"Mr. Harrington adds the skill of an engaged reporter, a personal stake in his subject and the ability to find fresh voices to talk openly about themselves and multi-racialism."
— *The New York Times* on *Crossings*

"This book is an example of what happens when a top-notch writer, laboring in solitude with purity of purpose, puts the right words in the right order."
— Madeleine Blais, Pulitzer Prize winner, author, *Uphill Walkers: Portrait of a Family* on *Acts of Creation*

"Walt Harrington's gracefully nuanced prose, full of feeling and finely observed detail, wonderfully conveys the world of craftsmen in all its artful integrity. In the grand tradition of Tracy Kidder, John McPhee and Joseph Mitchell, Harrington offers us a fascinating and enduring homage to men at work."
— Barry Siegel, Pulitzer Prize winner, director of the Literary Journalism Program, University of California, Irvine on *Acts of Creation*

# MORE BOOKS FROM WALT HARRINGTON

# MORE BOOKS FROM THE SAGER GROUP

See our entire library at TheSagerGroup.net

# THE
# DETECTIVE
## AND OTHER TRUE STORIES

## BY WALT HARRINGTON

With an Introduction by Alex Belth

THE
**STACKS READER SERIES**

Cover design and and cover art by WBYK.com.au
Interior design by Siori Kitajima, PatternBased.com

Cataloging-in-Publication data for this book
is available from the Library of Congress.
ISBN-13:
Paperback: 978-1-950154-65-4
eBook: 978-1-950154-64-7
Hardcover: 978-1-950154-72-2

Published by The Sager Group LLC
(TheSagerGroup.net)
In Cooperation with NeoText
(NeoTextCorp.com)

The Stacks Reader Series #007

# THE
# DETECTIVE
## AND OTHER TRUE STORIES

## BY WALT HARRINGTON

### With an Introduction by Alex Belth

*Dedicated to the memory of Matt Harrington,
my son and my friend.*

# CONTENTS

"Everything has gone to extremes," says D.C. Homicide detective V.I. Smith. Follow him into the front-line trenches at a time when Washington was known as the Homicide Capital of the nation, and you quickly see what he means—and understand the deadening weight of his sadness.

For Rita Dove, a former U.S. poet laureate, the writing of a poem is a curious, enlightening journey, an act of creation embedded in the mystery of art and the labor of craft.

Most Harvard grads go for the bucks and the prestige jobs. Bryan Stevenson is happy pulling down $24,000 trying to rescue convicted men and women from the death penalty. What makes Bryan go? "I feel the pleasure of God," he says.

For the Reverend James A. Holman, life has come full circle. In a sermon he once preached, he said, "Some people marry their cross. Some people give birth to their cross. And some people put their cross in a nursing home." So when their once-powerful father became too ill to care for himself, his daughters could see only one choice.

Rosa Parks was not a simple woman. She wasn't meek. She was

no more tired that day than usual. She had forethought aplenty when she refused to surrender her bus seat to a white man. We know it now as an American moment of awakening and reckoning. But the history of that moment is more complex.

George Herbert Walker Bush, the 41st president of the U.S., is today a well-respected ex-president and the father of a second generation of towering political figures. Yet, once upon a time, he was reviled as a whiny, waffling, boot-licking wimp? How did it ever come to this?

On having a long and fascinating acquaintanceship with the 43rd president of the U.S., a man who would become one of the most admired and, later, most reviled presidents in U.S. history.

What do fathers and sons see in each other? Themselves.

# PUBLISHER'S NOTE

Walt Harrington: A writer's writer with a strong moral compass, a compassion for others, and an abiding belief that all people are worth hearing, no matter how odd or foreign or even repulsive their views.

Perhaps it's not the most conventional way to open a testimonial about one of the most impactful journalists in our modern wave of creative nonfiction, but looking back, my first meetings with Walt Harrington unfold in my memory as scenes befitting a romantic comedy, perhaps something a little bit antic, penned by the great Nora Ephron, another journalist (and novelist and screenwriter) who lived in Washington, D.C., and had a great gift for telling human stories.

For me, writing has always been a matter of love, and finding ways to make it, and ways to ever improve. Though Harrington was not my first mentor, and not my last, he was by far my most influential.

My "meet cute" with Harrington was set in the *Washington Post* newsroom in the late fall of 1980. He was a hotshot writer from a smaller paper who'd come to interview for an open slot as an assistant city editor—as you might imagine, there was a steady stream of folks coming through the doors of the *Post*, looking to break into the bigs. As for me, I was entering my second year as a staff writer, promoted improbably from the ranks of the copy kids, which I suppose implied a little bit of hotshottery of my own. Ungracious as it may seem here, this little bit of self-congratulation becomes important to our story. Harrington was the master who taught me his craft; I was the sorcerer's apprentice. In all such tales, the resulting relationship goes one of two ways: great closeness—or the opposite. Four decades later Harrington and I are as brothers, united over long years by our shared pursuit of our singular missions, our dedication to our chosen form of art, our commiserations. To one another, we are the kind of family you choose.

Our first contact was actually no more than a glance . . . across a crowded room, sort of, though we were actually no more than three feet apart as Harrington was being shepherded to his next meet-and-greet. There was a strong and sudden connection. Dare I say we locked eyes? And then he was gone.

I don't recall any swelling music but there it was.

Cut forward a few months. It is 1981, and Harrington is hired by the *Post*. In newspapers, there are many different kinds of journalists who contribute to the mix. Some specialize in "just the facts, ma'am." They dig up city hall dirt and presidential corruption, and get to the bottom of local crime, politics, educational issues, and so forth. More recently there are other kinds who specialize in probing the internet or gathering data. In Walt's case, he was hired to be what might be called, in today's vernacular, a "writer whisperer," tasked with handling the kinds of staffers who were most inclined toward storytelling. In those days they called these types of articles "feature stories." I was assigned to Walt.

Any writer or editor knows the intensity of the relationship that can develop between these symbiotic partners. Whether it's a "one-story stand" or a long-time collaboration, editing is intimate. An editor gets inside your work, your ideas, your precious prose, your expense account. He is the sun by which you rise and set. The sun to which you make sacrifice. In time, some such teams learn to work beautifully together, like dance partners, like lovers, each spurring the other to greater performance, the two creating something that is more than the sum of its parts, which is pretty much the definition of Harrington's brand of journalism. I heard him say it a zillion times: You can give a bunch of reporters the same story assignment, and all will tell it differently. But very few will elevate the story into art.

We have our first meet-and-greet on a couple of semi-comfortable chairs designed to be a conference area, complete with a coffee table, set in an open space between the Weekly section and the Sports section, right in front of the "morgue"—an in-house, analog version of Google, also known as the library.

Walt has a folder of my work in his hand. I am 25. I have no idea of his age. He is, well, a grown-up.

Harrington proceeds to ask me if I've ever heard of a writer named Tom Wolfe. Seems he wrote a book called *The New Journalism*.

And that's when I realize I've spent the previous two years trying to reinvent the wheel. (And I guess nobody previously assigned to be my editor had recognized it either?)

My mind is blown.

In a way, you could say Walt Harrington gave me the gift of my own potential.

Like the journalism professor and department head he would later become, for the next year-plus I remained assigned to the City desk, he tutored me in the ways of a particular discipline he would later come to call *Intimate Journalism*—the title of his most influential textbook on journalism. He lent me books from his personal library; guided my reporting excursions into everyday life; and edited me line by line, gifting to my stories along the way an occasional literary flourish, as good editors sometimes will, no charge, the kind of fixes about which a writer *never* complains. One such early story would end up in a journalism text by another professor. Later, several of my stories would be included in Harrington's textbooks. That he thought of me as a suitable poster boy for his work, and collected me alongside more established writers, would greatly enhance my reputation. Of the hundreds of students and professionals he would teach, mentor, and lecture, I guess I was his first Frankenstein's monster.

Not only did he selflessly undertake my schooling, Harrington frequently took me home with him as well. I will never forget the delicious dinners cooked by his wife, Keran, at their cool apartment-with-a-loft space (which I would later inherit when their family began to grow), where I learned about jazz, arts and crafts furniture, and being a grown-up. With Keran's indulgence, Harrington and I talked craft and salacious office gossip deep into the evenings. Beneath Harrington's wisdom, enveloping it, permeating and informing it, is a wonderfully genuine humanness; if you tickle his funny bone, he'll guffaw and slap his thigh. Likewise, at the heart of Intimate Journalism is Harrington's strong moral compass, his compassion for others, and his abiding belief that all people are worth hearing, no matter how odd or foreign or even repulsive their views.

At the time we were working together daily, I was so engulfed by my own literary fire—fed as it was by the gasoline of Harrington's teachings—that I didn't realize how lucky I was to have this kind of attention. As it happened, I would much later learn, Harrington was only my editor because the *Post* didn't have a slot for a writer. He wanted a foot in the door at the great paper, and the editing slot was open, so he took it when it was offered. Though I had no idea about his past University of Missouri journalism schooling, his two master's degrees, or his intensive study of the craft (about which you can read in his interview with Alex Belth), he poured his knowledge unselfishly into me. As others share the inner glow of their religion, we shared the inner glow of our craft, and the special way he, and then I, have always sought to practice it.

Less than two years after we began working hand in glove, I was moved from the City desk to the Virginia desk—both of which, along with the Maryland desk, were part of a Metro section helmed by Watergate's Bob Woodward. I deployed my newfound skills as a roving correspondent in the far territories of our circulation, bringing back odd and wonderful little stories from an area that turned out to include my family's ancestral home.

While that move was meant as a promotion, clearly the result of my accomplishments under Harrington, there is a version of things in my mind where we were broken up as a team (at least in some measure) because we were getting a little too subversive for the old school newspaper people who ran the *Post*. Under Walt's command, as I started to deploy the techniques of Intimate Journalism he'd taught—scene, setting, dialog, character development, point of view, deep research, empathy, and the rest—I also came to learn that the conventional press was still, during the early eighties, a bit suspicious of this type of work.

In the minds of some, the artfulness of Intimate Journalism smacked of fabrication. Many veterans of the newsroom believed it was too good to be true, literally. And it turned out some of this worry was well-founded: Most infamous was the Janet Cooke incident at the *Post*, when a young reporter won the Pulitzer Prize and then shamefully had to return it when her story was revealed to be a fake. But Cooke didn't really practice Intimate Journalism or follow the rules, which began and ended with the journalism piece, the facts. In her case and others, the problem rested with the moral choices of the reporter.

Once, called into a superior's glass office to discuss my methods of employing dialogue in a story, Harrington jauntily invoked the spirit of Wolfe, who actually had spent two years as a *Post* reporter. "Tom Wolfe was doing this kind of stuff in the *Post* twenty years ago," Harrington said gingerly.

"Tom Wolfe was fired from the *Washington Post*," the editor replied.

Later, and for the first of many times, Walt ruefully quoted to me a favorite line from the jazz artist Louis Armstrong: "There's some people, if they don't know, you can't tell 'em."

I have lived by that philosophy ever since.

In 1983, after writing a number of outstanding stories for the *Washington Post Magazine*, (all freelance, on his own time, alongside his editing duties) Harrington became a full-time writer again. Feeling constrained, I left the paper in early 1984—an example, I guess, of the rashness of my youth compared with his maturity (and his growing family obligations). Either way, our friendship continued. In time, I'd be dumbstruck to learn that my mentor was only six years older than I.

For the next 14 years, as the *Washington Post Magazine* reinvented itself as a glossy insert, Harrington did scores of profiles of people both famous and obscure. He liked to say his goal was "to make ordinary people extraordinary and extraordinary people ordinary." And so he did. A selection of the best stories in both categories—eight articles—are collected here in *The Detective: And Other True Stories*, Harrington's eleventh book, sponsored by NeoText and brought to you by The Sager Group. I could not be more pleased.

One foundational lesson Harrington taught and practiced was that "journalism stories should not be a mere collection of facts. Instead, the stories should be about an *idea* the facts are used to illuminate."

In this spirit, the title story in this book, "The Detective," chronicles the moment-by-moment life of a Black homicide cop at a time when D.C. was the murder capital of the nation. But it is more than a gritty police ride along. It is also a story about the effect of the murder explosion in Washington on the psyche of the brave men and women on the front lines, and for all the rest of us watching at home on the TV news. Of note: many of Harrington's stories were directed toward understanding the inequalities of race and economics, a portent of things to come.

Harrington's profile of former U.S. poet laureate Rita Dove takes the reader through the looking glass of the exacting, protracted, ritualized, and intimate process of writing a single poem. But it is also a story about the ethereal act of creativity itself. The collaboration between these two master craftspeople makes for a beautiful story, a perfect marriage of subject with reporter, form with content, information with images and ideas.

In "The Mystery of Goodness," Harrington profiles a Harvard-trained lawyer who has dedicated himself to a $24,000-a-year job working to win freedom for men and women facing the death penalty. An examination of law and order and the penal system, it is also, at its deepest, an examination of human goodness and the power of Christian witness on others.

"The Reverend Comes Home" is a story about what happens when a once-powerful pillar of the community, too ill to care for himself, is taken in by his daughters at the end of his life. It is something we all face as humans, our parents' diminishment, followed by our own. What becomes important are not our accolades or community standing, but our family ties.

This amalgamation of fine detail and large ideas, Harrington says, "is at the heart of all fine journalism. We uncover the facts and find the deeper meanings. Otherwise, you are wasting your time and a reader's time."

Meanwhile, in his position at the *Post* magazine, Washington's "newspaper of record," which then published one million issues every Sunday, Harrington was thrown into the spotlight as he was tapped to profile a series of newsmakers and historical figures, including the Rev. Jesse Jackson, televangelist Jerry Falwell, Watergate reporter Carl Bernstein, and many others. Famous or obscure, Harrington's process was always the same.

No less a historical figure was the paper's executive editor, Ben Bradlee, who had guided the *Post* through its glory days of Watergate. Bradlee once told a gathering that Harrington's profile of a sitting vice president, George H. W. Bush, was the best political profile he'd ever read. Not lost In my memory—or Harrington's, I am sure—is the fact that high-up editors had resisted giving Harrington the coveted assignment in the first place, in lieu of one of the more established star political writers who gave the paper its reputation. *Who was this feature writer to dare stride in and represent the* Post?

After the Bush story, Bradlee made sure this milkman's son from Will County, IL, was well recognized among the staff for his worth, and compensated more on a scale with the others of his ilk. As time passed, Harrington would be asked to teach an in-house writing workshop. Over four years, scores of the best reporters in the country chose to attend.

Most importantly—at least to those who ascribe to the notions embodied by Intimate Journalism—President Bush *loved* the article that landed on doorsteps that Sunday morning. Soon, the liberal Harrington and his African American wife found themselves invited to movies and functions at the White House. A relationship developed. We have included his piece about that, as well.

As a bonus we also include a different sort of Harrington piece, a personal essay about fathers and sons. For my money, this is the sort of Harrington work that perhaps shines the brightest, the memoirs and essays gathered from the waters of his own life.

Over the past four decades, as Harrington moved from editing to writing to university teaching (and administrating), and then on to retirement a few years ago—I followed in his footsteps. As the master craftsman passed his knowledge to me, so have I passed it to others, and they to others.

Blending Harrington's methods with my own strengths, I was ever mindful of repping team Intimate Journalism, a brand that implied strenuous reporting, copious amounts of time spent, marathon transcribing sessions, and, above all, radical acceptance—an ability to see a world that is larger than you, a world that is complex and holds all kinds of competing ideas, with no true arbiter in apparent sight. Both Harrington and I have spent our lives walking miles and miles in the shoes of others. Along the way, we've tried, additionally, to place ourselves inside our subjects' minds and hearts. I know we both feel better for it, the life lessons having outlived the stories. And I'm pretty sure we both feel lucky to have each other to understand.

Each Harrington story is a precious gem. Like a valuable piece of woodwork or a beautiful song, they stand alone as totems of thought and ideas, artful and full of insight. Even through the decades, they still feel fresh. The meanings hold. By chronicling the ordinary lives of the famous and obscure with a hard-eyed compassion, he reveals not only the true natures of his subjects, but also the values they hold within the cultures they inhabit. In this way, his stories are as much about his readers as his subjects, a clue to understanding the conditions of others, something that could well serve our divided world of today.

And so, with this modest collection, we take great pleasure in sharing some of what this writer's writer has wrought. It stands as its own testament.

—Mike Sager
Editor and Publisher
The Sager Group

# INTRODUCTION

"The artfulness required to do intimate journalism is not mostly a God-given skill, but craft. It's crucial to think that way. Otherwise, we make the mistake of assuming that some people just have the knack. Some people do have the knack, but much of artful journalism, whether or not it is about ordinary people, is simply hard work."

— Walt Harrington in *Artful Journalism*

As was the case in so many areas of American life during the 1960s and 1970s, there was a revolution stirring in journalism: it would become known as the New Journalism, a genre that sought to intermarry stellar reportage—accuracy, fairness, and balance—with the literary elements of the novel—scene, setting, dialogue, physical description, and a narrative framework. Upstart magazines like *Rolling Stone* and *New York*, as well as alternative weeklies like the *Village Voice* and the *Boston Phoenix*, were most closely associated with this new style, but in the meantime, and perhaps a little more slowly, New Journalism forged a quiet but equally evocative path into the pages of mainstream newspapers as well.

As a newspaper reporter, and later, during the late 1980s and into the 1990s, as a staff writer for the *Washington Post Magazine*, Walt Harrington found his lane and flourished, creating his own brand of New Journalism, which would later be codified in a popular textbook. Authored by Harrington and published in 1997, *Intimate Journalism* was assigned for more than 20 years to thousands of undergraduate and graduate journalism students. Generations of longform writers working today have spent time studying the advice and techniques of this master craftsman.

During the early years of New Journalism, reporters and editors at newspapers questioned the form; they assumed that stories so well written and deeply insightful must have employed embellished truths and fictive storylines. Indeed, along the way, some newspaper *and* magazine writers betrayed that line of trust, none more infamous, perhaps, than Harrington's one-time *Post* colleague Janet Cooke, who was forced to return her Pulitzer Prize for Feature Writing after it was revealed that her story, about an eight-year-old heroin addict, had been fabricated.

Even so, the *Post* had been the first daily newspaper to turn its traditional "women's pages" into a Style section that would eventually feature some of the best newspaper writing of the times. By trusting its writers to express their creative voices in all sections of the paper, the *Post* created a hothouse for great storytelling that became a template for newspapers around the world.

Partly by dint of his modest character and middle-class, Midwestern upbringing—and partly due to the constraints of working for a glossy magazine housed under the flag of a newspaper so recently burned—Harrington developed a strain of New Journalism that diverged from the muscular egotism of early practitioners like Jimmy Breslin, Norman Mailer, and Tom Wolfe. Instead, Harrington—who received master's degrees in sociology and journalism from the University of Missouri—saw journalism through the humanistic lens of a sociologist.

Though some of his best-known work includes profiles of the famous (civil rights leader Jesse Jackson, poet laureate Rita Dove, Satanist Anton LaVey, religious right kingpin Jerry Falwell, civil rights pioneer Rosa Parks, and a then-sitting vice president George H. W. Bush, who would later invite the distinctly liberal reporter and his African American wife to the White House for a state dinner and movie night), the kinds of subjects who fascinated Harrington most were people (often Black) overlooked or undervalued by society and its cultural elite: a detective, a minister, an attorney who spends his life trying to save convicted criminals from the death sentences they face. As Harrington has written, "Unlike some stylishly interpretive journalism that aims to impose the author's 'attitude' on the

subject, my goal . . . is to be essentially self-effacing, to let interpreta-
tions arise from within the subjects themselves."

Harrington, the son of a milkman, was studying for his master's
in sociology at the University of Missouri, on the way to a doctorate,
when the Watergate scandal—which began when several burglars
connected to then-President Richard M. Nixon's re-election campaign
were arrested in the office of the Democratic National Committee,
located in the Watergate complex of buildings in Washington,
D.C.—caught his imagination. "I mis-spent a summer watching the
hearings in The Heidelberg Pub near campus since I had no TV,"
Harrington recalls.

Inspired by the heroic doings of Watergate reporters Bob
Woodward and Carl Bernstein, Harrington (like so many others of
his generation) became fascinated by the heroic potential of journalism to do good for society. He read Tom Wolfe's *The New Journalism*
when it came out in 1973, followed by David Halberstam's *The Best
and the Brightest* and John McPhee's *The Pine Barrens* and *Levels of the
Game*. He also started reading magazines like *Rolling Stone*, *The New
Yorker* and *Esquire*, long known for carrying the torch of literary journalism. "It wasn't long before I decided journalism looked far more
fun and interesting than academic sociology," Harrington muses.

While finishing his sociology master's degree in 1974, Harrington
started taking classes in journalism at Mizzou's lauded J school, and
he received his master's in journalism in 1975. Soon he became the
editor of the *Illinois Observer*; his stories there were good enough
to land him a job as a novice investigative reporter at the *Guide*, a
weekly investigative newspaper in Harrisburg, PA. An award from
the Pittsburgh Press Club, for best profile of the year, led to his next
job at the *Morning Call*, a daily newspaper in Allentown, PA. From
there, his stellar writing and more awards—from the Pennsylvania
Press Club for investigative reporting and the Lowell Mellett Award
for Media Criticism—brought him to the attention of the *Washington
Post*.

Harrington began at the *Post* as the features editor on the
city desk of the Metro section, which was headed at the time by
Watergate's Bob Woodward. Later Harrington returned to reporting,

and for fifteen years delivered immaculate and probing longform magazine feature stories for the *Post*'s Sunday magazine (including a profile of Woodward's former Watergate partner Carl Bernstein).

In 1996, Harrington traded his deep experience in the trenches (combined with his master's degrees) for a tenured position teaching journalism at the University of Illinois at Urbana-Champaign, in time serving as head of the Department of Journalism and as an associate chancellor of the university.

Meanwhile, Harrington went on to write books. His first, *American Profiles: Somebodies and Nobodies Who Matter* (1992), is a collection of his *Post Magazine* stories. *Crossings: A White Man's Journey Into Black America* (1993), which grew from a *Post Magazine* story about his biracial family, is a stunning work of reportage and memoir that foretold America's coming period of racial reckoning. *At the Heart of It: Ordinary People, Extraordinary Lives* (1996) would follow, featuring longform snapshots of everyday American lives, profiles of people like T. Deane Guy, a stock car racer; Jackie Jordan, a social worker in family services; and Sheri D'Amato, a girls' soccer coach, which are intended to be mirrors held up to the lives of readers.

Next came *Intimate Journalism: The Art and Craft of Reporting Everyday Life* (1997). The landmark textbook emerged from a series of writing classes he was asked by *Post* editors to present to staffers. Over four years, more than 100 reporters, all of them good enough to have been hired by one of the greatest newspapers in the world, took Harrington's classes in a voluntary quest to become better writers.

In 2002 Harrington wrote *The Everlasting Stream: A True Story of Rabbits, Guns, Friendship, and Family*. Published by the esteemed Atlantic Monthly Press, the deal was conducted personally with Harrington by the owner/publisher Morgan Entrekin, who continues to be a bold-face name in the industry. With *The Everlasting Stream*, Harrington enjoyed his widest mainstream success, a beautifully written and precisely reported memoir centered around rabbit hunting in the south-central Kentucky countryside with his Black father-in-law and his pals, and later also with his son, bringing three generations together in this ancient rite. (In the style of his icon McPhee, Harrington used a thermometer to record on various occasions the temperature of the stream in question; he also rigged himself up with a voice-activated recording device so he could make notes of impressions, wind direction, and other details while in the field with shotgun and camos.) In time the book was made into an elegiac Emmy Award-winning PBS documentary, for which Harrington was the screenwriter.

The success of *Intimate Journalism*, particularly the eloquence and passion of his take on the form, led Harrington-the-professor increasingly into writing about writing, and being invited to speak about "how narrative journalism gets done," as the ever-folksy Harrington likes to say.

*The Beholder's Eye* (2005) focused on the techniques for writing first-person stories. *Next Wave* (2012) sought to accent the continuing popularity of fine magazine writing at a time when death knells were sounding in the industry. Featured were a cast of up-and-coming writers, including Wright Thompson and Seth Wickersham, who have since become well known through their work at ESPN and on cable television. In 2013's *Slices of Life*, Harrington curates the artful journalism stories authored by students in his literary feature writing class.

Even while teaching, Harrington continued to have his hand in doing journalism, including a series of beautifully etched portraits of men and women who work with their hands for *This Old House* magazine. In 2014 those stories were collected as *Acts of Creation*. His most recent book, *Artful Journalism* (2015), is the work of a master craftsman at the height of his powers and knowledge, a collection of deeply insightful and evocative essays that have inspired and informed several generations of writers who aspire to do journalism.

*The Detective: And Other True Stories* features the highlights of Harrington's long and storied career, with looks at a Washington, D.C., homicide detective during the height of the homicide epidemic of the 1990s; the deeply considered art and craft of U.S. Poet Laureate Rita Dove as she works her way through writing one poem; a Harvard Law School grad who eschews a big-bucks job to make $24,000 a year trying to save convicted felons from death sentences; the trials and joys of a pair of sisters as they do their best to care for their aged, once-powerful father; an insider's look at the extraordinary life of civil rights pioneer Rosa Parks; a deeply reported profile of the 41$^{st}$ president of the U.S., George Herbert Walker Bush, followed by an account of the unlikely friendship Harrington developed with the 43rd president, George W. Bush, also known as Dubya. Finally, Harrington turns his thoughts inward with an essay about his own father and son, and the bridge between the generations.

—Alex Belth

**Alex Belth: When did you first get interested in writing?**

**Walt Harrington:** My older sister had been the editor of a high school newspaper. I was kind of a knucklehead and wasn't involved in too much stuff other than having a good time. The adviser to the high school newspaper called me in at the beginning of my senior year and said, "Your sister was the best editor we ever had here at this newspaper. And I want you to be the editor." And I said, "Well, I don't know how to be an editor." She said, "Your sister was really good at it. I'm sure you'll be good at it." Half the staff quit because I hadn't even worked on the paper. I edited the newspaper my senior year and had a wonderful time. Our investigation into glue-sniffing on campus and our investigation of the failure of the hall monitor system—we gave somebody a fake pass and they wandered around the halls all day long with a fake pass and nobody stopped them. I was always in the principal's office being yelled at for doing something in the newspaper.

**AB: Did you know you wanted to go to school and study journalism?**

**WH:** Not at first, no. I was going to work in a factory if I didn't go to college, so I took college—Blackburn College—seriously. I was going to be a lawyer because I came from a blue-collar family. My father's best friend was a lawyer and he always said, "You're smart enough to be a lawyer." So: I'll be a lawyer, even though I had no idea what that meant. But in college I fell under the wing of a sociology instructor. He was finishing his PhD at the University of Missouri and suggested I apply to grad school there. So I did.

I arrived in 1972 and was doing sociology for the first year. Then Watergate started to happen. Got my attention. Woodward and Bernstein, everything exciting was journalism at the time. And I thought, I'm going to go into journalism. And somewhere after my arrival, I realized the University of Missouri has one of the best journalism schools in the world. I applied for the master's program and got in. I finished my master's in sociology and then did an extra year to get a master's in journalism. In the journalism program I fell under the sway of another mentor, Ed Lambeth, who ran the Washington reporting program. In my last semester, in 1975, I went to the Washington reporting program in D.C. that was part of Mizzou. The whole program was breaking news, and I had no interest in breaking news. Everybody said you have to go work for the AP. You have to go work for the UPI. But again I had no interest in breaking news whatsoever.

**AB: What journalism were you reading at the time?**

**WH:** I had started to read *Esquire* and *Rolling Stone*, of course. Jimmy Breslin, Hunter Thompson, Gay Talese, Tom Wolfe. Later, Joan Didion. Also David Halberstam, especially his book *The Best and the Brightest*. And Robert Caro's book on Robert Moses, *The Power Broker*, and *Final Days* by Woodward and Bernstein. Reading these books I realized that journalism could be more than bureaucratic political coverage; it could actually be unraveling the human dimensions of power politics and policy.

**AB: How did you begin your professional career?**

**WH:** I had an old friend from undergraduate days who had taken a job as a researcher at this failing little political magazine in Springfield, Illinois. They couldn't get anybody to be editor of the magazine because it was only paying $165 a week. It was terrible. It was basically a kind of an advertiser rag for state legislators. He told me that if I came and would be the editor that I could do whatever I wanted. And so against everybody's advice, I did. But then I got a couple of traditional newspaper jobs—first in Harrisburg and then in Allentown—where I had a newspaper apprenticeship, covering everything.

**AB: Was the goal to write magazine features?**

**WH:** Well, I remember when I left the Harrisburg paper and went to Allentown. I was driving in the rain, two years out of graduate school, and I was going to be a Sunday reporter, which meant that I could do what would have been then called "takeouts" or what is known as "longform" today. You had a whole week to do a story. Wow. I became familiar with how ordinary life was meant to be examined and interpreted in profound ways. That's in the search for real meaning in ordinary life. I thought, well, I can write 20 articles that are each like a short story and I can collect those in a book. So even early on in those days, I thought in those terms. But it was a long time before I was able to put that all together because of the complexity of finding a place that will let you do it. It was easier in those days because newspapers were making so much money that they were willing to experiment in ways that they hadn't been in the past.

**AB: How did you get to the *Washington Post*?**

**WH:** So I was in Allentown for a year and a half. At one point, Don Nunes, a reporter from the *Washington Post*, came to interview for the city editor job at the Allentown paper. I was assigned to court him around, take him out to dinner, show him the town. He read my stuff and said I should be at the *Post*. I said I'd have to think about that. I did and applied. Shelby Coffey, the famous editor of the *Post*'s Style section, called me and said, "Well, your stuff looks interesting. If you're ever in Washington, come on in, I'd like to talk to you." Okay. It wasn't an interview. It was, come talk to me. So naturally I happened to be in Washington in the next few weeks. And I went in, I talked to him and he said, "Your stuff looks promising but I don't have any jobs." He told me to stay in touch and maybe something would come up. I'm walking out the door and this guy, Don Nunes, gets off the elevator and says, "What are you doing here?" I tell him I was just talking to Shelby about a job in Style but he doesn't have any. Don says, "We've been looking for a feature editor on the City staff for ages. They can't find anybody they want," he said. "Come on, I'll introduce you to the City desk." We go to the City editor and Don says, "This is Walt Harrington. Shelby Coffey is trying to hire him. But he doesn't have a job right now, so I think you ought to talk to him. So I talked to him for a while. Before long, I'm this kid that Shelby is trying to hire. And of course, he wasn't trying to hire me, but I didn't say anything. I came back in two weeks, went through a day of interviewing and they hired me. It was that fast.

**AB: How long did you work as an editor?**

**WH:** I edited at the *Post* from '81 to the middle of '83. I was on the Metro staff and we had wonderful people. Bob Woodward was the Metro editor. It was an intensely creative time, and there was a lot of freedom to experiment. Yet there were limits on what you could aspire to do. Then I went to the *Washington Post Magazine* and worked there as an editor. I wrote on the side and then within months I was just working as a writer. I wasn't editing anymore, but the only way I was hired at the time was because they had an editor's slot open, not a writer's slot.

**AB: It's true that money at newspapers enabled a certain kind of opportunity for you, but it also sounds like so much is good fortune and just dumb luck. Did you enjoy editing?**

**WH:** It was interesting. You learn to edit from a distance. You also have the experience of writers resisting you, and you have to stay open to the fact that those writers are correct. Sometimes, you're not always right. *They're* correct. Sometimes there's something that you're not seeing, or more likely in my own experience as a writer, it reveals that the writer has not done a good enough job of making clear what he or she is trying to do. Most writers have a switch that they can flick when they have to read their own work to try to edit it themselves. They still have a switch that they flip that allows them to step back a bit, but it's much more difficult to do for your own work. I enjoyed editing early on in my career. Since I didn't do it for that long, I was probably too heavy-handed. I wanted the writers to tell stories the way *I* wanted to tell stories—you know, especially for writers who maybe were not in complete control of what they were trying to do.

**AB: When you transitioned to writing, did you have a good relationship with your editors?**

**WH:** Anybody who is worth their salt wants a strong editor. A good editor asks questions. Asking: How do you know that? Do you really know that?

**AB: How were you able to apply the novelistic devices that are the foundations of New Journalism in a newspaper?**

**WH:** The wave of New Journalism made us aware of the possibilities. The other part was mastering the craft, figuring out how in the world do you get the good stuff and then make it seem like real life, of a life lived. Not some literary construct. That was always the undertaking, that was always the ambition, even though I wouldn't have articulated it like that at the time. Working for the *Post* it simply meant that you had to develop a set of absolute techniques. If you wrote that the gravel cracked under his feet when he walked, you had better have that recorded in your notes. When I later did *The Everlasting Stream*, it was still pre-electronics, I carried a compass with me and would record which direction the wind was coming from, checking my compass. That would be in my notes. Or if I had a tape recorder, I would talk into it and record where the wind was coming from. I learned all of this at the *Post*. In the early '80s, they moved lawyers into the newsroom at the *Post*. Lawyers would be in the newsroom asking you questions, and they're thinking of the courtroom three years from now—how is this going to look? In that environment, you really were attuned to being able to answer for your reporting. I never felt that was inappropriate. There were people who argued and fussed about it, but I was not one of them. I figured they were protecting me.

**AB: How did it inform your reporting?**

**WH:** In a way, it's almost like a self-fulfilling prophecy. When you work for a place where you have to verify everything as a reporter, you go forth on a story knowing how to collect information. And it makes you sharper and more attentive to details. And this kind of writing comes alive in dialogue, in inner monologue, in concrete details that all need to be reported and verified.

**AB: The kind of journalism you practiced is almost like an extension of your interest in anthropology and sociology.**

**WH:** Yes. The standard ethical stance of anthropology is first you absolutely do no harm to your subjects. In journalism it is: you tell the truth to your readers. And those two can actually conflict because sometimes the truth is going to harm the people that you're writing about. The answer in anthropology is, of course, anonymity. Sometimes that's the answer in journalism also. I mean, one of the things Mike Sager, with whom I worked at the *Post*, objected to most about mainstream journalism was the idea that you were almost never supposed to use anonymous subjects or sources. Mike's attitude was that three quarters of the world is stuff going on that people don't want anybody to know about, and we're not supposed to write about them? And so, you know, Mike would do things about upper middle-class heroin addicts but he didn't use their names. Of course those kinds of stories have the same problem that anthropologists have, which is—how do we know you're telling the truth? How do we know you're not making this stuff up? The whole reason to reveal your subjects and your sources is so that people can confirm and check them, you know? And in qualitative sociology and anthropology, you can't do that. Trying to do this kind of work at a place like *Washington Post Magazine* meant there was no room for slippage. There were a lot of straight news people who weren't too keen on this kind of stuff. They thought we were fancy pants trying to write these kinds of things.

**AB: You wrote freelance for other magazines outside of the *Post*. Did you either appreciate the *Post* culture more or did you get a sense of, wow, not everyone's that rigorous? Or did you find, uh, just different experiences, other places?**

**WH:** I didn't do a whole hell of a lot of freelancing, to be honest. I wrote for *Life* magazine and the editing process was very, very tight there. When you're getting good editing, it comes in layers. You get a conceptual edit. Then you start getting finer and finer gradations. And you're just really fortunate if you have somebody who really wants to pay attention. And someone who is not trying to hammer you or trying to bend you into something that they would prefer.

**AB: Have you enjoyed working as a teacher and passing along the tradition of narrative nonfiction to students?**

**WH:** Absolutely, it's been incredible. When I was in graduate school I was in a class—I don't remember what it was, exactly, probably advanced reporting or something. I was doing a story and wanted to make it special. And the teacher, a guy who had worked at a famous national newspaper, told me that I should probably find another career, that journalism was not for me.

And I can literally remember walking back to my apartment, leaving his office, it was pouring down rain. And I'm thinking, my God, here's this guy from a big-time national newspaper telling me to find another career, you know? Then I thought: He does not know what I'm trying to do. I don't know what I'm doing. I don't know what I'm trying to do, but he does not know what I'm trying to do. He's not helping me do what it is I want to do. He's trying to tell me I *can't* do it. And I had read enough to know that people did do it. He just didn't know it. So I've never, I've never used his name, but I always think about that. I'm never going to give a kid that kind of advice. I'm never going to tell a kid you can't do this or that. You try to help them figure out what are the opportunities for them, try and find what they want to do, and help teach them how to do this kind of work.

# THE DETECTIVE

"Everything has gone to extremes," says D.C. Homicide detective V.I. Smith. Follow him into the front-line trenches, at a time when Washington was known as the Homicide Capital of the nation, and you quickly see what he means—and understand the deadening weight of his sadness.

A man goes 22 years without being afraid, without giving his own death a glance, without worrying that the map of the city's criminal ways and rhythms that he has always carried in his head might be obsolete. A man goes 22 years climbing the ladder from beat cop to blue-boy elite, to homicide detective. A man goes 22 years to earn a reputation as a "90 percenter"—a detective who puts the souls of nearly all his victims to rest by closing the book on their murders. A man goes 22 years, and then the waters he inhabits shift and roil with unpredictable currents, until murder isn't murder anymore, isn't a biblical sentence that friends and lovers and fathers and sons impose on each other in storms of rage and recrimination. A man goes 22 years and finds himself leaning casually over a corpse on Halley Terrace in Southeast Washington, about to be made aware. That man—Detective Victor "V.I." Smith—flips back the dead man's coat and sees a blue-black machine gun, an Uzi, cocked and ready to fire.

Detective V.I. Smith is fearless, at least his police buddies think he's fearless. He has waltzed into Barry Farms, one of the roughest housing projects in Washington, at 4 in the morning, disappeared for an hour and returned with his suspect in tow. He has raided crack houses alone, lined up the drug heads and sweated them for reconnaissance on the spot. V.I.'s cop friends can't imagine him being afraid of anything. But tonight, after Halley Terrace, V.I. talks and talks about his shock at seeing that Uzi. About how six of his last seven murder victims have been packing guns. He doesn't reveal it to his comrades, but V.I. realizes that for the first time in 22 years as a Washington cop, he was afraid. Oh, maybe he'd been afraid before and hadn't realized it, imagined his feeling was excitement or readiness or the flow of adrenaline. But there's no mistaking or denying the emotion that surged through V.I. Smith on Halley Terrace tonight: It was fear.

Two years later . . . everything squeaks. The heavy doors squeak. The metal swivel chairs squeak. The drawers in the metal desks squeak. The file drawers squeak. The keys of the old manual upright squeak. The room—No. 5058, dubbed Homicide North because it is isolated two floors above D.C.'s other homicide offices in the city's Municipal Center—is a concerto of squeaks. Its other noises—the hollering voices, the clamoring phones, the electric typewriters, *Gilligan's Island* laugh-tracking on the beat-up TV, the two coffeepots spitting mud, the hand-held walkie-talkies belching static—all add layer upon layer of volume, creating finally a kind of jangled symphony.

What will stop this din and turn the entire room of nine men prayerfully silent are three words their ears are tuned to as if they were set on a private frequency: "stabbing" or "shooting" or "homicide." When the police radio dispatcher speaks any of these words, everything stops, hands reach for tiny volume knobs on radios and everybody waits. Usually, it's a false alarm and, just as abruptly, the noise once again envelops the momentary silence like a stadium cheer after the crack of a long ball.

The men in Homicide North are tonight "on the bubble"—cop talk meaning that their squad of detectives is on call to investigate the city's next murder. Detective Jeff Mayberry, a short, wiry, close-cropped, jet-propelled 34-year-old in a tight blue sports coat, is riding the top of the bubble in his rotation as lead investigator on whatever horror is next offered up from the bowels of the city. He has ridden the bubble aloft for four duty days now—and no murder. At least none on his 3-to-11 shift.

"You believe it?" he asks in frustration. No murder in a town that sees almost four murders every three days!

"You're bad luck," comes the rejoinder of his partner, Joe Fox, a respected and bearded 41-year-old bear of a detective who has a compulsive squint that constantly edges his wire-rimmed glasses up the bridge of his nose. He is called neither "Joe" nor "Fox." He is called "Joefox."

"Screw you, Joefox," Mayberry says.

Seated at the end of a row of desks in a corner under a wash of fluorescent light in front of pale curtains that hang off their track is V.I. Smith, looking out of place in this seedy domain. At age 46, he's quiet and self-contained, talking softly into the receiver of the old phone atop his desk, which isn't unkempt like most of the others. He's chatting with a woman who lives on W Street NW. She has been peeking out her window tonight to see if the drug boys V.I. wants to bust and shake down for tips about a recent murder are hanging on the street. They aren't.

Leaning on his elbows at his desk, talking into the phone, V.I. looks less like a tough city cop than, say, a prosecuting attorney or an FBI agent. He's 6 feet 4. Naked on the scale, he goes a trim and powerful 230, only 10 pounds over the weight he carried as a freshman basketball star at Howard University nearly three decades ago.

His face is wide and handsome, chiseled. It smiles rarely. In temperament, V.I. is terminally cool, never nervous or edgy. The more excited he gets, the more deliberately he speaks. And the more deliberately he speaks, the more trouble whomever he's speaking to is probably in. Even V.I.'s laugh is deliberate, with each "hah" in his slow "hah-hah-hah" being fully enunciated. In dress and style, he resembles a new-breed jazz player: His hair and mustache are short and neat, his shirt is crisp, his tie is knotted tightly and never yanked loose at his neck, and his suit, usually bought at Raleigh's, is always well-tailored and never cheap. Unlike some of his detective pals, V.I. would never wear brown shoes with a blue suit. He dresses to the nines because, having grown up on the streets of Black Washington, he knows that a man who dresses well is ascribed a dose of respect in that world, and every small advantage counts, especially these days.

The guys in the office call V.I. "the Ghost," because they rarely know what he's doing from minute to minute. With his reputation as one of Washington's best homicide detectives, V.I. comes and goes at Room 5058 pretty much as he pleases. But if the radio calls out a murder, he's on the scene, appearing as if from nowhere, like an apparition. Of Washington's 65 homicide detectives, V.I. Smith figures he's the only one without a regular partner. That's because Joefox, who came with V.I. to homicide seven years ago on the same cold Tuesday in February, used to be his partner, until the green and gung-ho Mayberry arrived from uniform four years ago and was assigned to Joefox for diapering.

Joefox and V.I. eventually took the kid aside and told him how it was going to be: The three of them would be partners, meaning that any one man's case was also the case of the other two. If Mayberry listened and studied and showed respect, he would learn the art and science of unraveling the darkest of human behaviors from two of the masters. And that's how it came down, with Mayberry now a fine detective in his own right. So when Mayberry is riding the bubble, Joefox and the Ghost are riding with him.

When the bubble seems to burst tonight, it's no thriller. A man named Willis Fields, who lived in a Washington boarding house, died at the Washington Hospital Center burn unit today, and the death was passed on to Detective C.J. Thomas, whose job it is to investigate and certify natural deaths. But in the hospital file he discovered that the 56-year-old man had told a nurse that "they" had poured alcohol on him and set him afire. Willis Fields was in the hospital 10 days, but his story fell through the cracks. Nobody called the police about his allegation, which means the inquiry will start nearly two weeks cold, no leads, only an address.

"C.J., why is it every one a these things you do, you always get us?" asks Mayberry. "Remember that guy on Suitland Parkway? Been there two years? Six shots to the head?"

"And what did you tell me?" C.J. asks.

"Man, that's a natural!"

"Well, here we go," says V.I., in his smooth, lyrical baritone as he palms a radio, unconsciously pats his right breast coat pocket for evidence of his ID wallet, pats his left breast coat pocket for evidence of his notebook, and heads out the door in his athlete's saunter, a stylized and liquid stroll, a modern cakewalk.

The address for Willis Fields is wrong—2119 11th St. NW is a vacant lot. "They probably got it turned around," V.I. says, as the threesome mills about the grassy lot, looking lamely around, shrugging. It's just before dusk and the hot summer day has begun to cool, but except for a man staring at them intently from the sidewalk in front of the Soul Saving Center Church of God across the street, the block is empty of people, quiet.

V.I. knows this neighborhood. He spent years living nearby as a kid, attending Garnet-Patterson Junior High over at 10th and U streets, Bell High School at Hiatt Place and Park Road and Cardozo High just up the hill at 13th and Clifton streets. This block of 11th Street isn't Beverly Hills, but it's a stable block that doesn't fit V.I.'s image of the crime at hand. An old man is more likely to be set on fire on a block where guys hang out drinking liquor, where there's a lot of street action. He nods down the road. That sounds more like the block back at 11th and U, with a corner market and a liquor store nearby. Sure enough, when the office checks the address the detectives were given, it's wrong. Willis Fields lived at 1929—near the corner of 11th and U.

Being in his old neighborhood makes V.I. nostalgic. As a boy, he seemed to live everywhere in Washington—Southeast, Northeast, here in Northwest, as his mother and father struggled and moved up from dumpy apartment to less dumpy apartment. Sometimes, he and his brothers sacked out four to a mattress. But in the '50s, V.I.'s daddy—a laborer by day, a cabby by night—bought a big old house on Adams Street in LeDroit Park, near First and W streets Northwest, and the kids finally slept two to a room.

The man who grew up to be a cop was no choirboy. He didn't worry about his grades, he cut classes to play basketball, he learned to palm loaded dice, he hustled pool. By age 16, V.I. was frequenting the now defunct Birdland and Rio nightclubs on 14th Street with his older buddies. And it was at one such club that his friend Jimmy got killed. They were hanging with a fool of a friend, who flipped his cigarette butt toward the bar and hit a dude in the neck. When the guy flicked out the narrow blade with the pearl handle, everybody scrambled, but Jimmy didn't scramble fast enough. He took the knife deep in his back, stumbled outside and bled out his life on the sidewalk.

After that, V.I. was more judicious about the company he kept. A lot of guys he hung with eventually went bad in the ways kids went bad in those days—stealing purses, robbing people on the street. But not V.I. For some reason—maybe because his daddy was so strict—V.I. was always afraid of the police. While other guys figured the cops would never catch them, V.I. figured the cops would always catch him.

One incident had frightened him good: A woman was raped in his neighborhood, and the police rounded up anybody on the street close to the rapist's description and took them to the old 10th Precinct. V.I. sat in a holding room until 3 a.m., when the cops told him he could go home—they'd caught their man. That night made V.I. a believer in the "wrong place, wrong time" theory of city life. A guy had to think ahead, anticipate, cut trouble off at the pass, stay off the streets and away from guys bound for infamy. Or go down too.

After a stint in the military, after attending Howard University, after becoming a basketball celebrity on the playgrounds of Washington and before graduating from American University, V.I. was sworn in as one of the city's early Black cops. Only a few days later, he attended the funeral of a boyhood friend, a kid nicknamed Porgy, a kid V.I. had learned to avoid. Porgy had graduated from purses to stickups, and he was killed in a gun battle with police. Almost 25 years later, V.I. has never stopped believing that with a few unlucky breaks, a few poor choices, he too could have gone down the toilet like Porgy. To this day, he can arrive on a street corner and find a young man who has just bled out his life on the sidewalk, and think:

But for the grace of God . . .

At 1929 11th St., nobody answers the door. So the detectives spread out and canvass the street, talking to neighbors. They have the office run the license plates of nearby parked cars, checking for the name Willis Fields. When an elderly man walks into the yard at 1929, Mayberry asks if he knows him.

"Yeah, I know 'im."

"When's the last time you talked to Willie?"

"The Sunday 'fore last."

"Who's he hang with?"

"He works at Ben's Chili Bowl."

"Where you live?"

It turns out the man lives in the room next to the one once occupied by Willis Fields. He says Fields has no girlfriend and few male friends, that nobody ever visits his room and that he smokes cigars and hits the bottle hard. The detectives want to get inside Fields's room to check for signs of a fire, because if he was burned in his room—fell asleep smoking and drinking liquor on the bed—it would show that he could have gotten burned on his back by accident, not malicious design. But the man says Fields's room is locked and that the landlady is out.

"What happened to 'im?" the man asks.

"He didn't tell ya?" asks V.I., careful to reveal no information likely to make its way into the street gossip mill.

"Hell if I know."

At Ben's Chili Bowl a block away on U Street, they ask their questions again. The whole time, V.I. is building scenarios, theories, in his mind. Say Fields had a buddy who often came to visit him at Ben's, but who hasn't stopped by in the last couple weeks. Good chance that guy knows something. Or say a woman always seemed to visit Fields on his payday. She's a good possibility. Or maybe Fields complained to a co-worker about somebody who'd been bothering him. Or mentioned somebody who owed him money. Whatever the story, V.I. knows from experience that men like Fields usually lead very simple lives. They go from their rooms to their jobs to the liquor store and back to their rooms. So that's the bird dog's trail.

Unfortunately, nobody at Ben's knows much about Fields either, except that he has been missing.

"Ooohhh, booooy!" says Mayberry.

As a murder, this case has "unsolved" written all over it. And unless V.I., Mayberry and Joefox declare it a homicide, it will likely be forgotten. There's been no publicity, no relatives or political heavy-weights demanding action. If Fields's death were declared a natural, his demise would slip into bureaucratic oblivion. It would't take up their time or mess up their statistics with an unsolved murder. It would—poof—disappear.

Except for one detail: Some dirtbag might have turned Willis Fields into a human torch, and catching the scum would bring great satisfaction. The idea is downright inspirational. Because in an era when most of the homicides V.I. gets are drug boys wasting drug boys, bandits beefing each other through the nose of a 9mm, or hotheads retaliating after some trivial insult, this Willis Fields case is, well, intriguing, a puzzle with most of the pieces missing. The men need to hit 1929 again, talk to the landlady, get into Fields's room. But in the meantime—since Willis Fields is still not an official homicide—Mayberry, Joefox and the Ghost are back on the bubble.

The call comes at 9:50 p.m. . . .

When the men arrive at Rhode Island Avenue and Brentwood Road NE, the scene, as it always does, seems not real, somehow outside of time and place, like a page brought to life from a paperback novel: The shooting ground is cordoned off in a triangle of yellow plastic tape (POLICE LINE DO NOT CROSS), and squad cars and cruisers are parked every which way, as if they'd landed as randomly as dice thrown in a tornado's game of craps. The crowd of mostly women and youngsters is congregated in the vague and dreamy light of street lamps beneath huge and gnarled trees in the scrub-grass yard of the L-shaped Brookland Manor apartments. A police helicopter flutters overhead, its searchlight scanning a block nearby. The cops know this stretch of Rhode Island as a drug market, and that's the first scenario V.I.'s mind starts to build. One shot, large caliber, left side of the head. That's all he knows.

V.I. steps into the triangle and begins to think in the language of the scene before him. On the sidewalk begins the pool of blood, not red, but a thick, syrupy black. The blood has cascaded over the curb and run southwest with gravity for about five feet, where a pile of leaves and debris has dammed its flow. The young man who was shot was alive when the ambulance left, but this is a large pool of blood, and V.I. figures Mayberry is off the bubble. On the sidewalk is a footprint in blood. Could be that of the victim, the shooter, a witness, a passerby, an ambulance attendant. A few feet away is a lonely quarter, heads up. On a waist-high embankment, where the sidewalk meets the yard about six feet from the street, stand a Mountain Dew bottle and a can of Red Bull malt liquor.

The details seem trivial, but a homicide detective's life is a sea of details, a collage of unconnected dots gathered and collated. In the end, most will turn out to be insignificant. But at the time, a detective cannot know the revelatory from the inconsequential. He must try to see them all, then hold them in his mind in abeyance until the few details that matter rise forth from the ocean to reveal themselves. V.I. begins to link the dots in the scene before him. For instance, a man who is shot at such close range was either hit by someone he trusted or by someone who sneaked up on him. Maybe the Mountain Dew and the Red Bull belonged to the victim and to one of his friends, who were sitting on the embankment looking toward the street, talking, laughing. From the darkened yard behind them the shooter moved in. The victim fell forward, his head landing at the curb and spurting blood with each heartbeat. His buddy bolted. If the dots are connected correctly, that buddy is a witness. If not, he could be the shooter.

Suddenly, from the crowd in the dreamy light on the scrub-grass yard, comes a long, awful scream. In five seconds, it comes again. And then a woman runs wildly through the crowd, crashing into people as she goes. She disappears into a door at the elbow of the L-shaped Brookland Manor. On the chance that this might be a drug-boy shooting, V.I., Mayberry and Joefox will not wander through the crowd or canvass the apartments looking for witnesses tonight. Until a few years ago, it was virtually unheard of for witnesses to be killed, but today they are crossed off like bad debts. Witnesses know it, cops know it, shooters know it. It's simply too dangerous for witnesses to be seen talking to the cops after a shooting, especially at night when the drug boys are out. V.I. plans to return tomorrow afternoon to do his canvass. But after hearing the woman scream, he invokes another law of experience: "You get people cryin', they gonna tell ya somethin'."

With this in mind, V.I. saunters toward the door at the building's elbow and the crowd parts and murmurs as he passes. On the darkened stairs up to the second floor, a place filled with the smells of a dozen dinners cooking, he finds the woman's mother, who says her daughter knew the victim but doesn't want to talk to the police. V.I. doesn't push. He gets the daughter's name, her apartment number. One of the problems these days is that victims and suspects are usually known on the streets only by nicknames that the cops don't know. So V.I. asks if the victim had a nickname. The mother says, "K.K."

The wanton killings of the last few years have changed everything. From 1964 to 1987, the number of Washington homicides fluctuated between 132 and 287, with 225 posted in 1987. In their first two years as detectives, the eager V.I. and Joefox drove around with their radio microphone in hand so they could lay claim to any murder as soon as it came down. Then, in 1988, homicides skyrocketed to 369—then 434, 474 and 483 in the following years, with the pace flagging only slightly so far this year. The police closure rate plummeted: By the end of 1991, only 65 percent of homicides from 1990 and 54 percent from 1991 had been closed by police, compared with 80 percent of homicides from 1986.

As homicides have gone berserk, so have the lives of V.I. and his fellow detectives. A cop used to have time to investigate his murders, interview everybody, build a case. In the old days, murder was more often a domestic affair, and a victim's killer was often found among his family. But by 1991, only 4 percent of Washington homicides were domestics, while more than three-quarters were attributed to drugs, robberies, burglaries, arguments or non-drug-related retaliations. All of which means that for most homicides today, detectives no longer have a neat list of identifiable suspects but a barrage of friends, enemies, business partners and competitors to investigate.

Even with more detectives, the cases are constantly rolling over one another, with new murders arriving before old ones are solved. Sometimes, V.I. sits down and pores through his old files so he doesn't plain forget a case.

And the drug-boy and bandit killings are so much more complicated than the old "mom and pop murders." V.I. has a case in far Northeast, where a bunch of guys opened fire on a crowd one evening, killing a young man and wounding three others. On its face, it looks like a drug-boy shooting. But the chain of events is also intertwined with the lives, loves, personalities and values of an array of individuals.

The case began, according to the tips V.I. has collected from informants, a week before the shooting, when a woman friend of a suspected drug dealer was beaten by another woman. The suspected drug dealer went gunning for his friend's assailant, but shot the wrong woman. A male friend of the woman who was mistakenly shot then interceded on her behalf with the shooter, who apparently took this as a threat. With several buddies, he sought out and killed the male friend of the woman who had been mistakenly shot, before the guy could ice him. And that's a simple case.

V.I. has had cases that intertwine with as many as a dozen other murders—shootings, retaliations, shootings, retaliations. He has cases where families have been wiped out. A young man was killed, and his brother was set to testify against the shooter and then the brother was killed. Another brother was set to testify against that brother's shooter and he was killed. A sister was set to testify against that brother's shooter and she too was shot. There's little moral outrage about many killings because of what V.I. calls "victim participation"—meaning the victims are often as sleazy as their killers. Nowadays, half the battle is finding some reason to lock up a suspected killer on another charge to get him off the street so witnesses will cooperate and so they will be safe. This onslaught has erupted in only a few years.

But that's not the worst of it: Worse yet is what has happened inside V.I.'s heart and his head. He goes to the home of dead kids these days, knocks on the door and tells a mother and father that their child has been killed, and they say, "Yeah, okay." Without a hint of emotion, they close the door. The homicide detective's code of honor has always been that he identifies with the dead, swears to find the killer. These days, that's harder and harder. It's hard to get worked up over the injustice of a dead man who may have killed one or two or three people himself.

But that's not the worst of it: Worse yet is that V.I. has had witnesses he promised to protect get killed. After he promised! So, after 24 years of putting his honor and duty on the line at any time, night or day, V.I. Smith stopped promising. He began saying only that he would do what he could. He has been forced to make his own moral choices outside the expectations of the law: He has let murderers stay free rather than risk the lives of more witnesses.

But even that's not the worst of it: Worse yet is that in the last few years, V.I. Smith—tough, cool, brave—has ridden home late at night and broken down in tears of private bereavement: The fabric of the city where he grew up, the city he loves, has been shredded, destroyed. People on the outside haven't grasped this yet, haven't felt the deadening weight of this sadness, this heartsickness.

From Brookland Manor, V.I. takes only a nickname. He is famous for crashing cases at the scene, not waiting until tomorrow to investigate. He theorizes from the dots and pushes every lead to the limit. He can't interview witnesses tonight, but maybe the detectives dispatched to the hospital have a lead he can push. Maybe a brother or the mother or father of the victim named names, knew somebody who was beefing with the victim, gave the cops a line. V.I. heads back out the door, through the parting crowd, to see what Mayberry and Joefox have learned.

"He's gonna live," Mayberry says.

"That right?" V.I. asks without emotion. He glances at the pool of blood: KK is one lucky dude. Then he heads for his cruiser. He will not spend one more millisecond connecting the dots of this picture.

It is an attempted murder now, another cop's glory, another cop's worry. They are still on the bubble . . .

At 1929 11th St., the landlady is home. She seems to stop breathing when they tell her Willis Fields is dead. With her hands covering her cheeks she leads the detectives up an oddly tinted turquoise stairway to his dowdy, sweltering room. One life, one room. A round white clock on the wall reads 10:55. On the dingy carpet lie one razor blade, a bottle cap and a few toothpicks. Half a dozen shirts hang on a rack, along with a single pair of pants, dirty. A lamp without a cover, an unmade bed, a small bottle of Listerine, nearly empty, three unopened bars of soap, a loaf of Wonder Bread. On the wall are a calendar and a newspaper photo of a woman in black hat, underwear and stockings. Atop the television are three pens, a pencil, a nail clipper, a wristwatch, six cigars and two packs of matches. On the nightstand is a red address book. In it are the names of people listed as owing Fields money.

"Whatever happened didn't happen here," says V.I., which means the death of Fields is probably a murder. V.I. starts theorizing, figuring maybe Fields went on a drinking binge and demanded money from one of his debtors, who went off. Lighting someone on fire isn't an efficient way to kill; it's more a murder of passion. As the detectives are about to leave, call it a day's work at 11:35 p.m., the landlady's brother arrives.

On the last Saturday of Willis Fields's life, the brother says, he had come out of the apartment he shares with his sister, headed to catch a plane for vacation. He found Fields passed out drunk on the exterior steps going up to his room. He mentions two men—Robert and Theodore, whom Fields often hung out with on the street. He talks for a long time and the detectives are about to leave when the brother, in an aside, says, "He was layin' right there in the doorway, and this old fag was tryin' to frisk him." Mayberry, Joefox and V.I. look at each other in wonder at what people can forget to mention.

"You know his name?" Joefox asks.

"Naw, he be down the street."

"Did Fields go in the house then?" V.I. asks.

"Stump can answer that," the brother says, explaining that he left Willis Fields in the care of one of Fields's friends, who happened along the Saturday before last, a man nicknamed Stump. V.I. knows that none of the people mentioned or interviewed so far tonight is a suspect, and he figures Stump isn't either, but a trail's a trail. He says of Stump, "That's where we gotta start."

For days more, Mayberry, Joefox and the Ghost are on the bubble. Amazing! Still no murders on 3-to-11. Just the luck of the draw. But when a man and his squad are on the bubble, it's hard to do much police work, because when the call comes, everything else must be dropped. V.I. has nonetheless arranged for the squad to squeeze in a quick raid one night, sweep in with some uniformed cops in marked cruisers and hit the drug boys hanging on W Street, where his source is still peeking out the window and reporting back. Two guys argued on that street a while back and one ended up killing the other. At least that's how V.I.'s informants have explained the murder, but he has "no eyes"—no witnesses willing to testify.

His plan is to sweep in, make everybody hug the ground, scare up some guns and drugs, drag the crew downtown and start sweatin' 'em about the murder. When a guy's looking at five-to-ten on a federal firearms rap, his memory can improve dramatically. Very little planning goes into such a raid. Eat some pizza, watch the Redskins, or *Top Cops*, or *Road Warrior*—then hop in the cars and do it. Although V.I. figures maybe a quarter of the guys on that street will be strapped with guns or have a gun hidden nearby, no detective will wear a bulletproof vest. All in a day's work. But night after night, the drug boys don't cooperate, and the street stays empty. Word comes back to V.I. through the drug boys' girlfriends that pals of the dead man are planning a retaliatory drive-by shooting and everybody is staying scarce.

While on the bubble, V.I. works his case in far Northeast. He conspicuously cruises the neighborhood, which is a signal to his informants that he wants them to call. V.I. will collect reconnaissance as well as spread rumors—gossip that will get more people talking so his real informants will have cover, gossip that may make the shooter fear his own friends and allies are turning against him. Some guys will flag down V.I. in the street and talk to him. These are young men who have their own troubles with the law and who can tell their friends they were discussing their cases, asking V.I. to put in a good word with a judge or a prosecutor. V.I. often does. But the way the game is played, he wants payback—the names of potential witnesses, the name of a shooter, the details of the Byzantine events that often lead up to a killing.

"You owe me big time," V.I. tells one young man.

"That last thing didn't work. They done me."

V.I. is unmoved. "I can't save you twice. But I did it the first time. So stay in touch. I can make it worth your while. I gotta get some eyes."

It seems that nobody helps the cops anymore just because it's the right thing to do. "You ain't got nobody helpin' ya now," V.I. says. "Nobody gives a crap. You gotta make everybody do what you want 'em to do. And you gotta be real mean to get results." The drug-boy killings have spooked everybody. V.I. can't blame folks. But that has meant more and more of his encounters with potential witnesses are hostile.

More and more, he has to threaten people to get their coopera-tion. He has to get them subpoenaed before the grand jury and then warn them that they can be charged with perjury if they don't tell the truth. And these are innocent people. He has even hinted that a witness's name might leak out before a suspected shooter has been jailed, unless that witness agrees to testify after the guy is locked up. He must sometimes act threatening to even the most harmless of people, which is what happens on the Saturday afternoon V.I. swings by the home of the last man known to have seen Willis Fields alive. Stump, a 64-year-old man whose real name is Earl Johnson, is off his porch and headed for his front door the instant V.I.'s cruiser pulls to the curb. V.I. halts the retreat.

"Need to talk to you. Detective Smith, Homicide."

"You wanta come inside?"

"No, sir, you gonna have ta come with me." V.I. opens the creaking front-yard gate and gestures toward his cruiser.

Stump is disoriented. "I gotta tell my wife."

"You can call her from downtown."

"I don't know nothin'."

"We gonna just talk about it."

"I don't know nothin'."

Stump looks up at his wife, who is peering down from a second-story window. V.I. could have interviewed Stump at home, but he believes people are a lot like animals: They're more comfortable in their own territory. He wants them uncomfortable, so they drive off toward the station. Suddenly, the word "stabbing" squawks from the cruiser radio. "You got a condition?" V.I. asks the dispatcher.

"I didn't do nothin'," Stump says from the back seat.

"Hey, Stump, we know you all right, man." V.I. says this in a more friendly tone, trying to calm the man down. Then he heads for the scene of the stabbing, doing 85 mph on the Southwest Freeway. He arrives at M and Half streets SW. The victim is gone and only a dab of blood stains the sidewalk. He will live.

Still on the bubble . . .

Seated back at Homicide North, staring into the middle distance and wringing thick and worn hands, Stump is not a happy camper. He's a short man with a good belly, a mustache and short graying hair. He wears his blue-and-white cap backwards. He wears blue work pants and a white short-sleeved shirt. A ring of keys hangs off his belt.

"Never did a crime in my life," Stump says to the air.

"You know Fields?"

"Right. But what happened to him, I don't know."

As these things often go, however, Stump knows more than he knows he knows. He says that before the detectives came around asking questions, a man nicknamed Bo had told him that Fields had been set on fire. V.I. knows from the hospital report that an unidentified person drove Fields to the hospital. He figures Fields must have told that person what happened. And he figures that person might have told others.

"You can't set me up for no murder," Stump says.

"I'm not tryin' ta charge you with murder," V.I. says, knowing that indeed Stump is not a suspect. "Did you ask Bo how he knew Fields got burned?"

"He said it was over on 18th Street."

"Did he tell ya who Fields was with?"

"He never did tell me that."

"How'd he know about it?"

"I don't know."

"You know who lives up on 18th?"

"I don't."

V.I. then takes Stump out cruising the neighborhood for Bo, but they don't find him. "I wanta go home," Stump says.

"That's where we're on the way to."

Says V.I., "Bo is the next guy to talk with."

Back at the office, V.I. finds Joefox and Mayberry yukking it up. As V.I. has been working the fringes of other cases while riding the bubble, they too have been working other cases. Joefox is telling about his informant who called and said his mother was sick in another city and that he needed $300 for airfare to visit her. He said he hated to be a snitch, but that his mother was very sick. Then he gave Joefox the address of a shooter Joefox was after. Even before patrolmen could make the arrest, Joefox's informant walked into the office looking for his finder's fee.

"They're still out tryin' ta get 'im," Joefox said.

With that, the informant picked up Joefox's phone, rang a number and asked for the shooter by name. They chatted. "See, I told ya he's still there," the man said after hanging up.

"Man, they got caller ID?" asked an incredulous Joefox.

"Ah, I don't think so."

Anyway, the cops got a shooter, the informant got his cash, and, presumably, a sick mother got a visit from a devoted son.

It's unimaginable that Mayberry, Joefox and the Ghost won't draw a murder tonight, Saturday night. But in the meantime, before the intrigues of darkness set in, V.I. heads out to Northeast Washington to meet Detective J.O. Johnson. They're off to look for Tony Boyce and Eldee Edwards, who are wanted for obstruction of justice for allegedly threatening a witness scheduled to testify in a grand jury investigation into a murder in which Edwards is a suspect.

The detectives cruise East Capitol near 17th Street, where Tony lives. They hope to find him on the street. It's safer to make an arrest outside. Besides, if they raid the men's homes and come up empty, the men will learn the cops are on their tails and maybe take an extended vacation. V.I. interviewed Tony a couple days ago, hoping to get him to give up his buddy Eldee, but Tony hung tough. He told them to bug off, that if they were gonna arrest him, then arrest him. And call his lawyer. He wasn't tellin' 'em anything. V.I. let Tony go. But he doesn't like it when cops are treated rudely, and he's back today with a warrant. Because it's late afternoon on Saturday, there will be no judges available to process Tony's case until Monday, which means he'll cool in jail for at least the weekend. When they finally spot Tony walking up East Capitol, V.I. pulls a U-turn and hops out.

"How ya doin'?" V.I. asks in a friendly voice.

"I'm fine," says Tony, momentarily confused. He's a short, thin 31-year-old man wearing a white Champion T-shirt, bluejeans shorts and lavender Saucony running shoes. He has a dark blue wrap on his hair. His nails are long, his body lithe and taut.

"I got a warrant for ya."

"For my arrest?"

"Yep."

V.I. is downright cheerful. He gently turns Tony toward the trunk of a car, has him lay down the leather-bound Bible he's carrying and clamps the cuffs on him behind his back. A man walks up and gruffly asks what's happening.

"They arrestin' me!" Tony says, emotional now, with an edge of fear in his high-pitched voice. "I don't know why."

V.I.'s entire manner changes. "Sir!" he says to the man in a deep and suddenly ominous voice, stepping toward him with the full authority of his 230 pounds. "You wanta walk wherever you walkin', because you gonna be the next one that's locked up." The man opens his mouth to speak, but before the words emerge, V.I. says, "Walk wherever you walkin'! I don't wanta hear 'bout it." The man does not move, and V.I. goes stone calm. "Turn and go," he says in almost a whisper. "Turn and go." And the man does. Just then, a woman arrives and says she is Tony's mother. Because she is polite, because a mother has the right to worry about her son, V.I. is polite in return.

"I'll call you," he says.

After Tony is taken away in a paddy wagon, J.O. and V.I. head for the last known address for Eldee Edwards. Now that Tony has been taken, there's no hope of surprising his friend. J.O. goes to cover the back door and V.I. climbs the steep steps to the row house's front porch. To his right is a gray cat sunning itself on a stone railing. To his left, beneath a striped awning, sits an old man in a green metal chair. V.I. asks if he has seen Eldee, and the old man nods.

"Where's he at? In the house?"

"No."

"When's the last time you saw 'im?"

"Two days ago, three days ago."

"Who's home now?"

"My daughter."

"How old's she?"

"Forty."

Walking into a strange house is a dangerous play, and V.I. has asked the old man these questions as reconnaissance. He believes the old man is telling the truth, although he has learned not to rely too heavily on his intuition in such matters because any cop who thinks he can't be successfully lied to is a fool. V.I. has been tricked more times than he cares to remember. "Lookin' at a jail sentence," he says, "makes people great liars." He knocks hard on the door eight times. No answer. He waits, opens the door, knocks hard nine times and hollers, "Hello!" No answer. He walks in the door. A narrow hallway leads back to a kitchen, rooms are off to the left, a stairway rises on the right. On the floor are two unopened gallons of fresh paint.

The place brings a flash of déjà vu, because it was in just this kind of house that, as a young uniformed cop, V.I. had decided to play hero when he got a report of a burglary in progress. When nobody answered the door in the darkened house, he didn't announce that he was a policeman for fear of warning the burglar, and he walked in. When he flicked on the light, he looked up the stairway to see an old woman huddled terrified on her knees and an old man standing resolutely with a shotgun aimed down the stairwell's tunnel at the intruder—Patrolman V.I. Smith.

"Hello!" he hollers again, and his voice rings like a trumpet in the cavernous hallway. No answer. He waits four seconds and hollers "Hello" again. He waits six seconds and yells, "Anybody home?" He waits five more seconds and yells "Hello," louder this time. His back pressed against the wall, his gun still in the holster, he starts slowly up the stairs. As he goes, he glances calmly back and forth from the first to second floors. Finally, a woman appears on the upstairs landing, and V.I. introduces himself as a policeman.

"I'm looking for Eldee."

"Eldee has not lived here in four or five years," she says, seeming miffed at the question.

"How frequently you see him?"

"Maybe three times a week."

"You got a phone number?"

"No. He lives in Southeast. That's all I can tell ya."

J.O. Johnson has joined them in the foyer now, and he isn't happy with what he's hearing. "I talked to you the other day myself, and I had a little confidence in what you was tellin' me, but now you make me think that you're not bein' truthful."

The woman starts to interrupt, "You know . . ."

J.O. cuts her off, "We're tryin' to be nice about it."

The woman snickers.

"We haven't been here at 4 o'clock in the mornin' and wake everybody up in the house and turn the house upside down lookin' for Eldee. I'm sure you don't want us to do that."

"I don't think that you supposed to be doin' that."

"You don't know what we supposed to be doin'. I'm askin' you to get in touch with him and have him call me. Tonight."

"Okay," she says, clearly angry.

In the car, V.I. says, "He's probably in and outta there."

"I can tell ya one thing," J.O. says, "when I break back in here 'bout 4 o'clock in the morning . . ."

Says V.I., "She doesn't believe."

When Eldee doesn't call later that night, J.O. will take his warrant and a crew of cops and hit the last known address of Eldee Edwards in the early morning hours. He will get everybody out of bed, secure them downstairs and search for Eldee. He will not find him. But afterward, V.I. will figure the folks in that house will be more likely to lean heavily on Eldee to turn himself in. They will have been made believers.

But right now, back at Homicide North, V.I. looks straight into the eyes of Tony Boyce, who is sitting with his right elbow on his knee, his chin on his fist and his left hand cuffed to his chair. V.I. says nothing. He gets a cup of coffee, checks the score of the Eagles-Jets game on the tube. Then he reads Tony his rights and tells him he'll be arraigned Monday morning.

"Monday morning?" Tony asks, shocked. "Does my lawyer know?"

V.I. asks Tony if he has his lawyer's phone number.

"Not here."

V.I. shrugs.

"Why didn't you arrest me yesterday?" Tony asks, finally realizing that he'll spend at least the weekend in jail.

V.I. shrugs again.

After the paperwork is done and Mayberry takes Tony, who has abandoned his cool and loosed a blast of obscenity, down to a cell, Joefox says, "He'll have a lotta company down there."

"Saturday in the big house!" says V.I. And then, out of character, he throws back his head and roars with laughter.

Incredibly, 11 o'clock comes and goes. They are still on the bubble

. . .

Over the years, V.I. has had some spectacular cases. Soon after he came to Homicide in 1986, when he was barely off the natural death detail, he solved a series of killings in which a man in a dark van was abducting women and murdering them. The 7-year-old brother of one dead woman had mentioned to V.I. that his sister kept her boyfriends' phone numbers on the back of matchbooks and that they were spread all over the house. V.I. had the boy collect them in a bag, and the next day he began calling numbers, posing as a doctor tracking a case of venereal disease. After 17 calls, V.I. found a man who had seen the woman the night she died. Before the day was over, V.I. had interviewed him, discovered the name of another man the dead woman had been with that night, located his dark van, and gone with his squad to arrest him.

Just last winter, V.I. and Joefox were assigned by Chief Isaac Fulwood Jr. himself to handle a high-publicity multiple murder on P Street NW, in which a man, woman and child were found slain in a car. They were a brother and sister and her 2-year-old son. When the body of the child, who had been suffocated, was taken from the back seat, it looked to V.I. as if the boy were only asleep.

He felt the righteousness rise in him, felt his revulsion for the random injustice, felt as if this could happen to his own family, his own friends. There was no "victim participation." And when V.I. and Joefox went to the home of the dead to inform their parents, who were also the boy's grandparents, the family cried, sobbed as humans should, must, if they are to be human. V.I., Joefox and Mayberry, the entire squad, worked day and night for four days. As their reward, as affirmation of their own humanity, they locked up the alleged son-of-a-bitch killer, who's now awaiting trial and facing the possibility of life in prison.

That's what has changed. So many murders seem to count for nothing today. They don't embody the eternals of love and devotion and loss, recall the immeasurable value of one life, no matter how seemingly insignificant, announce through quick justice that living is safe and predictable and violence an aberration, thereby cauterizing the psychic wounds of the living. No, these murders trumpet the evil, insidious reverse: Life is cheap, easily forgotten, humanity is a fraud. At the front lines of this diminution, V.I. Smith feels his own humanity under assault, feels the fire of indignation in his belly going cold. His deep fear is that, at the front lines, he is taking only the early hit for an entire society. Because what's happening to V.I.

Smith is happening to everyone who reads the paper or watches the TV news. His numbed heart is but an early warning.

"If you see the motives for why people are killing people out there now, you say to yourself, 'How can you do anything about somebody who's thinkin' like this?' It's valueless. You go into a crack house two or three months after it's got rollin' and find a family with young girls 15, 16 years old who have lost everything. They've lost their dignity. They've lost their will. They've lost themselves.

"And what have you accomplished being a policeman? You're on TV: 'We got one of the biggest cocaine raids we've had and locked up two New Yorkers.' But you've left the victimized family devastated and haven't given them any alternative. But I don't have time to worry about people anymore. And it's a goddamned shame.

"I've gotten to the point where I'm not really comfortable doing what I do anymore. I've gotten to the point where I sense fear. And I've never done that before. You can't predict who's out there anymore. Everything has gone to extremes."

On the next 3-to-11 shift, with Joefox home sick, the bubble finally bursts at 5:30 p.m., probably too early for a drug-boy killing. On the way to the scene in an apartment on 29th Street SE, just off Pennsylvania Avenue, V.I. starts theorizing. Female victim, inside her apartment, shot once in the head. When a person is killed inside her home, the case is usually easier, because it's a snap to discover the last person to see the victim alive. It's also daylight, which makes any investigation easier still, and, most promising, this killing is in a normally quiet neighborhood, which hints at an old-fashioned, mom-and-pop murder, a murder of passion. When Mayberry and V.I. walk into the door of Apartment 101, they find half a dozen cops, like gawkers at a car crash, milling around. Mayberry orders everybody out.

The dead woman is lying in the middle of the room, halfway between the front door and the rear patio doors, one of which has been knocked off its track. It is an ugly scene, with brain and skull splattered on the wall and floor. The room is dark, but they don't touch the light switches for fear of smudging any prints. They wander the apartment with flashlights and find a framed photo of a woman. Mayberry flashes a light on the dead woman's face to be certain it is her.

In a matter of minutes, the dots are made whole: The woman, Crystal Johnson-Kinzer, and a male friend had walked in the door and been attacked. The male friend had escaped as shots were fired. The woman did not. Outside the patio balcony, detectives scouring the yard and garbage cans for clues find a footprint with a distinctive circle in the tread imprinted on the hood of a gray Toyota parked beneath the balcony.

When the victim's family arrives, there is—as there should be—great anguish. For months, they say, Crystal had been harassed by her husband, from whom she was separated. She'd quit a job, moved across town to this apartment, gotten a court order for him to stay away. Crystal's brother is screaming at the police: "She called y'all! And now look! Y'all come when it's too late!" He is weeping and hitting his forehead with his fist. Crystal's father, wearing the gray uniform of a working man, stands perfectly still, stunned silent. Her mother, with a rose bandana wrapped on her head, shuffles about without expression, wiping her face again and again with a tissue. The fiancée of Crystal's brother—a woman who is a look-alike for Crystal, a woman who was often mistaken for her twin—is holding a diapered baby and sobbing.

Amid this horror, V.I. is invigorated, renewed. This poor woman! She could have been his sister, his daughter! A sweet 22-year-old girl with a good job as a telephone operator. She loved smooth jazz, John Coltrane. She was studying cosmetology at night. She came from a nice, protective family. She'd stopped at her apartment to change clothes and head out for a picnic at her brother's. She does not deserve this. This murder is "real"—with a good guy and a bad guy. Crystal's death must be avenged. Says V.I., "You don't get many like this anymore."

Back at Homicide North, the details are gathered and collated, family and friends are interviewed, the husband's undistinguished police record is pulled. At 12:17 a.m., V.I. has finished writing the arrest warrant for Kodie Cotrell Kinzer, age 21, last known address in Silver Spring. It's the home of Kinzer's grandmother, and V.I. figures it's probably where he ran to, because that's just what shooters usually do.

"They wanta go home," V.I. says.

"We gotta start the hunt!" says Mayberry, excited.

When they arrive at the Georgetown home of the judge who will sign the arrest warrant, V.I. notices for the first time that it is a lovely, perfectly clear and starry night, cool, with a light breeze. The Georgetown street is quiet, except for the soothing mantra of crickets and the conversation of what look to be two drunken college boys stumbling home. As V.I. walks through the manicured garden courtyard to the judge's town house, he sees yard after yard marked with signs that read "Electronic Security by Night Owl." It's the kind of neighborhood V.I. hasn't seen much of in his job. As the judge puts down his book and reads the warrant, V.I. studies the high, elegant ceilings in the judge's home. "You wouldn't be needin' our services too often in this neighborhood," he says, and the judge laughs.

The Montgomery County police are waiting for the three-car caravan of detectives that arrives about 2 in the morning. Taking down a suspected murderer is still an exotic event in suburban Montgomery, and the sergeant on duty is talking about whether he should call in the SWAT team and waiting for a captain to arrive to take responsibility for the decisions.

"They don't get to do this much," Mayberry whispers.

"It's comin'," V.I. answers ominously. "Believe me, it's comin'."

Despite the delay, the detectives will not complain. V.I. doesn't want neighboring police telling stories about how Washington's cowboy cops came out and broke protocol or acted arrogant. So they wait . . . and wait . . . and wait. Finally, it is decided that several more cars of Montgomery cops, all of whom don bulletproof vests, will surround the apartment, and V.I. will call in on a telephone and announce the raid. This gentlemanly approach runs against every grain in Mayberry and V.I., who back home would take a couple of uniformed cops and knock on the damned door.

On the phone, V.I. talks to a young man who says Kodie Kinzer isn't home and that Kinzer's grandmother is too frail to be awakened with the shock of a police raid. V.I. asks the youth to come outside, which he does. He's a very nice kid, clean-cut, polite.

"Did you see Kodie last night?" V.I. asks gently.

"I came in like late, 'bout 1 or 2."

"Was he in bed?"

"Yes, sir."

"Where does he usually sleep?"

"Huh?"

"Where does he usually sleep?"

"He sleeps on the couch."

"He doesn't have a room?"

"No, he's like a pass-through."

"You know of any girlfriends he might be stayin' with?"

"I couldn't tell ya."

"How old is Kodie's grandmother?"

"She's 'bout 70."

"Is she in pretty good health?"

"Ah, not really, that's why I say I didn't wanta scare her."

"Do you expect him to come back tonight?"

"Uhm, I don't think so."

"Why not?"

"Huh?"

"Why not?"

"Ah, 'cause, ah, he was, uhm, talkin' about he was gonna go over his friend's house or somethin'."

"You ever meet his wife?"

"Nah, I never met her. I heard of her name before."

V.I. looks at Mayberry. "Think we oughta wake Grandma up?" Mayberry shrugs, but he is thinking of a line from the movie *Dirty Harry*: "I gots ta know." And he knows V.I. is thinking the same thing. The kid seems honest, but V.I. has learned not to always trust his intuition. They didn't come all the way out here with seven, eight police cars to be talked away at the door. V.I. is being gentle, getting the kid used to the idea.

"Captain, whataya think?" V.I. asks, bringing the Montgomery brass into a decision that he has already made. The captain nods, and V.I. turns back to the youth. "Think it would be a problem if we talk to Kodie's grandmother?"

The young man looks suddenly shaky. "See, all those people . . ."

V.I. cuts him off. "There ain't gonna be all those people."

"I don't, I don't know . . ."

V.I. cuts him off again, this time in a voice that has once again gone stone calm: "Look, man, this is somethin' we gotta do. Prolongin' the situation isn't gonna do any good. Let's go."

Inside, buried beneath a pile of blankets, they find Kodie Kinzer. Minutes later, he's led away, his head tilted downward mournfully. He's wearing yellow shorts, a white T-shirt, white socks and no shoes. When V.I. leaves the apartment, he's carrying a pair of black Adidas with three white stripes adorning the uppers and a distinctive circle on the sole. It will be up to Forensics to evaluate whether they could have left that footprint on the car beneath Crystal Johnson-Kinzer's balcony. But V.I. says, "I remember that tread."

It is nearly dawn by the time V.I. and Mayberry finish interviewing Kodie Kinzer, who denies that he killed Crystal. When the detectives head back to Homicide North, leaving Kinzer in a Montgomery cell awaiting extradition to Washington, the city is just waking up. The sky is brightening in the east, and people are standing at bus stops in twos and threes. A laundry truck is picking up, a Coke truck is dropping off, and the lights of sleeping cars are awakening along the roads. Outside police headquarters, a rat scurries along the sidewalk, stops, gazes about at the emerging daylight and dives into the bushes for cover.

Life as it should be.

In the next few weeks, V.I. will keep tugging at threads in his murder case in far Northeast—the one that began when a suspected drug dealer shot the wrong woman. Before that chain of misery and foolishness concludes, five people will end up shot. He'll keep working the murder of Willis Fields, never finding Bo, the man who told Stump that Fields was attacked on 18th Street. But no matter.

Bo was simply repeating street rumor passed on by lots of other people. V.I. will discover that somebody who lives on 18th Street owed Fields money. But it will be a long time, if ever, before that murder is avenged. In the meantime, Tony Boyce will stay in jail for weeks and be indicted for obstruction of justice. Eldee Edwards will be arrested and indicted for murder. In a few days, Kodie Kinzer will arrive at the D.C. Jail, where he will await trial after his indictment for murder. Soon, Mayberry, Joefox and the Ghost will collect half a dozen new homicides, all of which will look like drug-boy killings.

But that's all in the future. This morning, just back from the hunt, V.I. and Mayberry still have their damned paperwork to do. And in Room 5058, the coffee is cold, of course. But that's okay. It has been a good night—an old-fashioned night, a night that affirmed the world's predictability, justice and humanity, that healed the psychic wounds of the living, that again brought feeling to the numbed heart of Detective Victor "V.I." Smith. This horrific night has made him feel better. It has made him feel human again.

# A NARROW WORLD MADE WIDE

For Rita Dove, a former U.S. poet laureate, the writing of a poem is a curious, enlightening journey, an act of creation embedded in the mystery of art and the labor of craft.

"Bed, where are you flying to?"
—A line jotted in a notebook in 1980 by Rita Dove,
United States poet laureate

*ebruary 5, 1995, 5:35 p.m.*

Twilight is not the time Rita Dove prefers to work. Much better are the crystal hours between midnight and 5 a.m., her writing hours when she lived in Ireland the summer of 1978, before her daughter was born, and Rita was young, with only a handful of poems published, before the Pulitzer Prize, before she became poet laureate of the United States. In Ireland, she and her husband, Fred Viebahn, a German novelist, would spend the late afternoons selecting dinner at the fish market, filling their sherry bottle from the merchant's oak cask, strolling Dublin's streets. They would cook dinner, write letters, read, talk, make love, watch TV into the late night, and then Rita would write, or do what people call writing, until the milkman arrived at sunrise and it was time to go off to sleep.

No more, not with her 12-year-old daughter, Aviva, the trips to Washington, the phone and fax, the letters, speeches, interviews, the traveling—oh, the traveling. It's the worst. It doesn't respect a poet's frame of mind. Rita can't go off chasing a shard of thought about the three-legged telescope her father once bought, or why it is that hosts in southern Germany fill up a guest's wineglass before it is empty, or whether a forest's leaves can be both mute and riotous at once (they can, of course). While traveling, Rita must catch a plane, look both ways, always muster the dedicated, logical mind of a banker or a plumber.

But this afternoon, for the first time in a while, she sits at her desk in her new writing cabin, which stands down a sharp slope from the back door of her house in the countrified suburbs of Charlottesville, where she teaches at the University of Virginia. The cabin is small—12 by 20, a storage shed with insulation and drywall, a skylight so tiny it's more like the thought of a skylight, a wall of windows whose mullions create miniature portraits of the woods, pond, mountains and sunset to the west. No phone, fax, TV, no bathroom or running water, hardly any books by others and certainly no copies of her own nine books: "They're done. They have nothing to do with the moment of writing a poem." On a small stereo, she plays music without words—lately, Bach's Brandenburg concertos and Keith Jarrett's jazz piano.

The last few days, Rita has been thinking about three poems she'd like to write—"Meditation," "Parlor" and "Sweet Dreams." She began to ponder the last poem after she reread a few lines she'd scribbled in a notebook in 1980. For 15 years, she had looked at those lines every couple of months and thought, "No, I can't do it yet." She wrote 300 other poems instead. But just seven weeks from today, Rita Dove will consider "Sweet Dreams" done—with a new title, new lines, new images and a new meaning the poet herself will not recognize until the poem is nearly finished. It will be a curious, enlightening journey: one poem, one act of creation, evoked from a thousand private choices, embedded in breath and heartbeat, music, meter and rhyme, in the logic of thought and the intuition of emotion, in the confluence of the two, in the mystery of art and the labor of craft, which will transform random journal notations, bodiless images, unanchored thoughts, orphan lines of poetry and meticulously kept records of times and dates into something more. Words with dictionary meanings will become words that mean only what the experiences of others will make of them, words no longer spoken in Rita's voice but in whispering voices heard only inside the heads of those who pause to read her poem.

In 1980, living in a $50-a-month, one-room walk-up in West Berlin, Rita was sick in bed one day. For light reading, she picked up *Das Bett*, a German book about the place of the bed in history. She was leafing page to page, when she came upon this sentence: "Vergleiche man die Waende der Wohnung mit einer Nusschale, so waere das Bett jene feine Haut um den Nusskern, den Menschen."

She stopped. She loved the sentence, its meaning—if the walls of an apartment are like a nutshell, then the apartment's bed is like the fine, delicate skin around the kernel, which is the human being. But she also loved the sentence's sound. In the way that the sensuous glissando of a harp, the haunting blue note of a trumpet or the hypnotic percussion of a drum can touch a person's mood, Rita's mood was touched by the sound of the German words said together in their sentence. As a composer might hear a bird twittering and a woodpecker pecking and suddenly hear instead a melody, Rita suddenly felt "the cadence of thought."

The sentence said something beautiful and it sounded beautiful: "And that is the essence of poetry." It is language as idea and sensation at once: "the clay that makes the pot." She copied the German sentence into her notebook and wrote, "Bed, where are you flying to?" She imagined the bed as a home, the bed as a magic carpet, the bed as a world: "That's the inspiration. I have no idea what the leap is."

Soon after, she wrote:

**sic itur ad astra**
(such is the way to the stars, or to immortality)

Bed, where are you flying to?
I went to sleep
an hour ago, now
I'm on a porch
open to the world.

I don't remember a thing,
not even dreaming.

and Chagall shall play
his piebald violin.

we'll throw away
the books and play
sea-diver in the sheets—
for aren't we all children
in our over-size shirts (clothes),
white priests of the night!

Rita enjoyed the lines, especially the first stanza. Like the sentence in *Das Bett*, it seemed to have a music all its own and to carry the exuberance and spontaneity of a child's dream, although the stanza also baffled Rita: "I wasn't quite sure what it meant."

Rita has, after a fashion, a filing system—plastic folders in yellow, blue, red, purple, green, pink, peach or clear. She doesn't file her nascent poems by subject or title, as a scientist or historian might file documents. She files poems by the way they feel to her. Red attracts poems about war and violence. Purple, Rita's favorite color, accumulates introspective poems. Yellow likes sunshine. Blue likes the sky. Green likes nature. Pink—after a line she wrote about her daughter: "We're in the pink/ and the pink's in us"—is a magnet for poems about mothers and daughters. But the categories aren't fixed: Blue is the color of sky, but blue is also the color of the Virgin Mary's robe.

Rita's flying bed poem went in the clear folder, which holds very little: "The clear folder wants to be pure thought." A perfect, clear, pure lyrical poem: "It was a daunting folder. Very few things ever made it out of that folder."

But when Rita sits down at her desk this 5th of February, as she goes through her ritual of laying out her folders, looking at each and waiting for the door to her intuition to swing open and reveal to her which she should pick up and thumb through, she reaches for the clear folder, reads the old poem and thinks: "Maybe I can do it now." Maybe in this cabin, clean and fresh and pure as a lyrical poem, she can finally finish it.

"It was now or never."

At 5:35, she writes:

**SWEET DREAMS**
   —*Sic itur ad astra.* (Such is the way to the stars.)

Bed, where are you flying to?
I went to sleep nearly
an hour ago—now I'm on a porch
open to the stars!

I don't remember a thing,
not the crease in the sheet,
the neighbor's washing machine.
I'm a child again, barefoot, catching
my death of cold,

in my oversized nightshirt
and stocking cap . . .
but so are all the others,
eyes wide, arms outstretched in greeting—
white priests of the night!

Rita is fiddling, playing, just seeing where her mind takes her words. She has changed the poem's title to "Sweet Dreams." She has lost Chagall and his piebald violin, the sea-diver in the sheets. She has gained the neighbor's washing machine, the crease in the sheet and the barefoot child catching her death of cold. She has altered punctuation. But as she rereads the poem, it is the stanza she wrote 15 years ago that grabs her—the porch open to the world has become the porch open to the stars: "It changed without me even thinking about it." What did that mean? She jots these notes on her poem: "The original impulse of the poem—it was meant to be magic, pure impossible magic. The speaker goes to sleep & wakes into a journey—is it a dream or the lost feeling when you wake & don't know where you are? . . . How to capture the ecstasy, the spontaneity?"

Rita now enters a strange and magical place in the creation of her poetry, as she begins to carry on a kind of conversation with her poem, as she tries to actually listen to what the poem she has written is trying to tell her, the poet.

And the poem begins to create itself.

Rita uses this analogy: One of her favorite books as a girl was *Harold and the Purple Crayon*. With his crayon, Harold drew before him on the blank page the places he wanted to go—a street, a hill, a house. He created the world into which he then entered. But once inside that world, it was real, not an illusion. For Rita, writing a poem is like Harold drawing his way through life: Once a line is written she can step out onto it. The line is like a train and she a passenger curious to learn its destination. Each line is an idea that carries her to the next idea. Yes, she is taking the poem somewhere, but the poem is also taking her.

Some people's minds run from point A to point B with the linear determination of an express bus roaring from stop to distant stop. Theirs are minds trained to avoid detours, to cut a path past the alleys and side streets of distraction. Rita's mind is more like the water of a stream swirling randomly, chaotically and unpredictably over the stones below as it still flows resolutely downstream: "It's hard to describe your own mind, but I am really interested in the process of thought. Sometimes I catch myself observing my own thoughts and think, 'Boy, that's kinda strange how that works.' " Rita is not like those who see tangential thoughts as distracting digressions: "I'm interested in the sidetracking."

When her poem's first stanza was written, for instance, its character was in a dream, flying on a bed, feeling a child's excitement—"open to the world." Perhaps, Rita asks herself, she unthinkingly changed "world" to "stars" in a later version not as a simple slip of the pen, but because the world is really what her dreamer wants to leave behind? Perhaps the stars—or immortality, the word Rita wrote beneath the poem's title 15 years ago—are her character's real destination? And, she tells herself, that isn't just exciting but also frightening, meaning that "Sweet Dreams" was never meant to be only a joyful, childlike poem.

"That's what had stopped me all these years."

*February 10, 4:30 p.m.*
In her cabin, Rita stands at the *Schreibpult*, the stand-up writing desk that her father, an amateur woodworker, built as a surprise for her two years ago when she turned 40. While visiting her folks, Rita saw the desk in their basement. She came upstairs and said to her father, "That's a pretty nice desk down there." And he said, "Well, when your birthday comes you can take it home." It had been a decade since Rita had mentioned to her father that she'd like such a desk: "It was astonishing."

Rita is sick today, coughing and feverish, but the jobs of wife, mother, professor and poet laureate go on, with the job of poet taking a back seat. It has been a satisfying and grueling time that will ease this summer when her two-year tenure as laureate expires, but the fame that it has brought will forever change her life. She can no longer write in her university office, because someone will stop by to visit. She can no longer sit in an outdoor cafe in town and read, because someone will recognize her. Some days she hasn't the time to make a single entry in her notebook—not a fragment of conversation, a recipe, a fresh word. She has a new book of poetry just out, *Mother Love*, but still feels a creative emptiness in the face of so many demands, is afraid of losing the human connection to the clay that makes the pot: "It's harder and harder. Fame is very seductive. I'm tired of hearing the sound of my own voice. I want to be silent." Often, she has asked herself, "Was I writing for prizes? No. I wrote because of those moments when something happens in a poem." She once wrote these lines: "He used to sleep like a glass of water/ held up in the hand of a very young girl."

"That was a great moment."

Rita loves the image, although she doesn't know exactly what it means or even feel the need to know. She remembers a line written by poet Stanley Kunitz: "The night nailed like an orange to my brow."

Kunitz once said that for years he lived in fear that someone would ask him to explain that line. He didn't understand the image, Rita says, but he wasn't going to touch it. "Sometimes you have those moments. Those are the moments you live for. There are some that change your life. When I write, I feel like I am learning something new every second. But I'm also feeling something more deeply. You don't know where you've been. That's the mystery of it. And then to be able to put it down so that someone else can feel it! I feel incredibly alive."

Outside Rita's cabin windows, two Canada geese are nesting at the pond beneath the little pier Fred built last year. Never before has she had so comforting a view from the windows of a study. The years she and Fred spent in Europe, they lived in dark apartments that looked out onto concrete. In Arizona, she gazed out at a decaying swimming pool in the back yard.

This cabin is doing something to Rita. When she was a 10-year-old girl, a few months before her first period, she daydreamed a house for herself: "It was small, one room . . . This dream house would stand in the back yard, away from the house with its clinging odors but close enough to run back—just in case." Her cabin is eerily reminiscent of the fantasy. And like Harold's purple crayon, like a poem that begins to create itself, the cabin is casting its own role in Rita's life. When she comes here, even for an hour, she writes at least a line or two. In this cabin, even in the middle of the day, it seems like the crystal hours from midnight to 5 a.m.

"It's a harkening back."

On her desk, Rita has put the tiniest clock she could find, and she has decorated her bulletin board with pictures. A photo of a Colorado sand dune that resembles the torso of a woman: "I just love this. I don't know why I love it." A postcard depicting a solarium (her grandmother's house had a solarium) in which sits a violoncello, an instrument Rita played as a girl: "It's a room I'd like to be in." A snapshot of Rita and her daughter, who is almost totally obscured by shadows, standing in a dry riverbed in Arizona: "You can barely see her, but I know she's there." What do the pictures mean? Rita has no idea. "These are things that make me start to dream. They open my mind."

She writes in her journal: "What I love about my cabin—what I always forget that I love until I open the door and step into it—is the absolute quiet. Oh, not the dead silence of a studio, a silence so physical that you begin to gasp for air; and it's not the allegorical silence of an empty apartment, with its creaks and sniffles and traffic a dull roar below, and the neighbors' muffled treading overhead. No, this is the silence of the world: birds shifting weight on branches, the branches squeaking against other twigs, the deer hooshing through the woods . . . It's a silence where you can hear your blood in your chest, if you choose to listen."

*February 20, 5:45 p.m.*
Rita has identified her problem: She's like an opera singer who must—without exercising her voice, humming a bar, hearing a note struck on a keyboard—hit a perfect B-flat. She has been away from the first stanza of "Sweet Dreams" so long, she likes it so much, that it's like one of her published books—it's *done*. She can't read the lines and rekindle the emotions that created the lines in the first place—and so she can't hitch a ride on those emotions into the rest of the poem. In the language of the poetry craft, she can't "make the turn" from the first stanza to the next. So she ignores the first stanza, begins without it.

In her cabin, she writes:

> I'm a child again, barefoot,
> catching my death of cold
> in a nightshirt I've never seen before
> fluttering white as a sail . . .
>
> moonlight cool as peaches above me,
> below,—but I won't look below.
>
> Bed, come back (here), I need you!
> I don't know my way back.
> Bed, at least leave me my pillow

Rita is writing lines and stepping out onto them. She decides to break away from "the tyranny of the typewritten page." In the margins, at odd angles, she writes: "purple crayon," "blow," "languid," "fluid," "landings," "whispering, happy landings." She is searching for the feeling of flying. Suddenly, she's frustrated: "Can I fly? If I could only remember! How does one remember?" She continues to scribble: "I've lost my feet," "with its garden of smells," "aromas," "crushed smells," "its petals whispering happy landings." She picks up a book of poetry by Wallace Stevens, thumbs through the pages and jots down words that strike her: "confusion," "hermit," "fetched." She scrawls: "purple hermit of dream."

At 6:02, she writes:

> I'm a child again, barefoot,
> catching my death of cold
> in a nightshirt I've never seen before
> fluttering white as a sail.
>
> Above me, moonlight cool as peaches.
> Below . . . but I won't look below . . .
>
> Come here bed, I need you!
> I don't know my way back.
> At least leave me my pillow
> with its crushed aromas, its
> garden of dreams, its purple petals
> whispering *Happy landings*

"*I'm a child again.*" Too explanatory. The poem should have the feeling of childhood without needing to announce it.

"*Catching my death of cold.*" It goes on too long. This poem must be a collage of fleeting images, as in a dream. But Rita likes the line and would like to find a way to keep it.

"*Moonlight cool as peaches.*" She likes that line, too, may use it someday in another poem, but to mention food while in flight is too corporeal, too earthly. Still, she'll leave it in for now.

*"In a nightshirt I've never seen before."* The image is too surreal, gives the sensation that the poem is a real dream rather than the sensation that it is like a dream.

*"I won't look below."* Not believable. Her poem's character wouldn't need to remind herself not to look below at the world. She's yearning to leave it behind—for a ride to the stars.

*"Come here bed, I need you!"* Wait, the poem is talking to Rita again: Its traveler is ambivalent about her journey. She craves the stars but, like a child, also the comfort of her bed.

*"I don't know my way back."* The word "back" is too narrow, too referential to the world. This traveler isn't worried about the way "back," but the way to the stars, the future, immortality.

*"Garden of dreams," "purple petals," "Happy landings."* "Yech!" "Awful!" "Disgusting!" But Rita doesn't stop to change them. They are place holders for the poem's cadence. New words will come.

On and on it goes—each line, each word examined. At 6:10, 6:15, 7:33 and 7:44, Rita begins new versions. She now believes that the complicated emotions in her poem can no longer be described as "Sweet Dreams." She hates it that people always accuse poets of being "hermetic"—hard to understand, obscure—but she goes back to the original Latin title from 1980 anyway. Unlike an essayist, who must keep in mind readers' tastes, interests, biases and education the better to convince them, Rita never thinks of her readers: "That sounds awful, I know. But to me a poem can't possibly be honest if I'm thinking about my readers."

It is a paradox: Rita has a better chance of reaching the emotions of her readers if she doesn't consciously try to reach them, if she doesn't worry about how people will respond to a certain poem. Pondering that would put a kind of emotional membrane between herself and her material, making it less authentic and more distant from the unmediated emotion she is trying to feel and then evoke, reinvent, in her readers: "If I start thinking about the world and about the reception of this poem in the world, then I'm lost. I'm lost. It's not gonna be a poem."

Rita deletes "crushed aromas" because the word aroma is too "thick," not simple enough. That allows her to replace "garden of dreams," a cliche, with "garden of smells." She likes that change, because a smell, unlike an aroma, can be either pleasant or sickening. "Purple petals," which probably referred back to Harold's purple crayon, is excised. It's, well, too purple. Now, without "crushed aromas" and "purple petals," she adds "crushed petals." She plays with the poem's enjambment—the way sentences run on or break from line to line—looking for meanings that she didn't see at first: "Catching my death/ of cold in a fluttering nightshirt," for instance, can mean something far different from "catching my death of cold/ in a fluttering nightshirt."

At 7:44, with Keith Jarrett playing, she writes:

### SIC ITUR AD ASTRA
*—Thus is the way to the stars.*

Bed, where are you flying to?
I went to sleep nearly
an hour ago, and now
I'm on a porch open
to the stars—barefoot,

catching my death of cold,
in a fluttering nightshirt
white as a sail. Above me,
moonlight cool as peaches.
Bed, come back here,

I need you! I don't know
my way. At least leave me
my pillow, with its garden of smells,
its crushed petals whispering
*Lay back. Relax. Gentle landings.*

On the poem she jots: "dreams" and "worries of the day," reminding herself not to lose the poem's dreamlike feeling and to add the idea that traveling to the stars is also a way to leave the trivial bothers of daily life behind.

*February 24, 5:35 p.m.*

In her journal, Rita writes: "I want more intriguing, surprising metaphors . . . I want the language to imitate the clarity of children's literature . . . I'm looking for an image as wild and apt, as wonderfully penetrating yet impenetrable, as Gabriel Garcia Marquez: '. . . and death began to flow through his bones like a river of ashes.' If I could catch a fish like that, I'd be ready to die. No, not really. But the contentment would be immense and would last my entire life."

But not so others can read the line and admire her as she admires Marquez, but so she can feel the line's creation. It's an addictive joy, a feeling of exhilaration, yes, but not of pride. It's beyond pride, or maybe before it: "I feel very humble: 'Thank you, line. I don't know where you came from, but you're greater than I am.' You have those moments. They're the ones that keep you writing. You're always after the next fish."

It is 6:20 now, sundown out the cabin window. Rita takes up a new pen and writes: "Now we'll see how this pen works. Sungown. Dundown. The light quenched. Oh, fennel bloom. Another ladybug— perennially cute, ladybug, body and name. Too many make a plague of luck. Ah shame on you, duckie: You've lost your quack. For an ounce of your prattle I'd hang up my traveling shoes."

What does it mean? Who knows.

Gone fishing.

*March 13, 4:23 p.m.*

Rita was going through old notebooks earlier today, trying to unclog her mind, searching for inspiration hidden in a line or even a word: "A word that will knock this damn poem back on line." It was a beautiful 73-degree day outside, but Rita was at her desk imagining the sensations of flying on a bed at night: "The absence of incidental 'white noise,' the smells and the cool feelings that night floats up in us, almost like the earth is emitting a faint subterranean sigh."

She wants to write this poem, but the world is relentless: *USA Weekend* has asked the U.S.A. poet laureate for an original poem to publish, she must plan her laureate's farewell poetry reading at the Library of Congress, organize the panels for an upcoming literature conference, write the opening remarks for the Nobel Laureates in Literature convocation, finish writing her lecture for the university faculty colloquium and write the foreword to an anthology of stories written by children. That's for starters. But then, going through a tiny black and red notebook, Rita comes across a snatch of forgotten poetry she jotted down while at a conference in Morelia, Mexico, in January 1994.

### READING BEFORE SLEEP

Bed, where are you flying to?
One minute ago I climbed
    into the cool
waters of night & now
    (end of day)
I'm on a porch
open to the sky
    world!
If I close my eyes
I'll sink back
into the day, made
    strange —
but no, my eyes are open
and I am falling it
    seems
forward

Rita is amazed. Just the other day, she made a note to remind herself to add to her poem the idea that traveling to the stars was also a way to escape daily life—"the worries of the day." Now she finds, in the forgotten Mexico notations, these lines: "If I close my eyes/ I'll sink back/ into the day." She thinks, "This thing has been haunting me for all these years." She writes in her journal: "Somewhere there's a few lines about melancholy . . . Where is that sheet of paper?" Then, dutifully, she spends the afternoon and the evening working on a poem for *USA Weekend*.

*March 17, 5:47 p.m.*

Fred has asked Rita to go with him and Aviva to the stable where Aviva keeps her horse. Rita, who hasn't been out to the stable in months, hears Fred's plea and agrees, although she plans to sit in the car, watch Aviva and her horse trot around the track and work on "Sic Itur." But once she gets to the stable, she can't capture the poem's mood. The grounds are too much of the earth, not the stars. So Rita works on "Parlor," one of the three unfinished poems she considered working on way back on February 5. She works for an hour, scribbling additions and deletions and notations on her copy. Then Fred climbs into the car, out of the cold, and turns on the radio news.

"Does that disturb you?" he asks.

"No," Rita says, lying. "I think I'll just stretch my legs."

Walking out along the fence line in the descending darkness, Rita asks herself, "I've had all this time to write. Why can't I give up this few minutes?" She wants to be in her cabin writing, but she wants to be with Fred and Aviva. She wants to be with Fred and Aviva, but she wants to be poet laureate of the United States: "I want to fly as a poet." She takes out her notebook and writes, "Sic Itur Ad Astra: You don't want to come down. Immortality—it's loneliness. You long for the pillow's smells, the earth you are leaving but that's all you can take—the recycled breath, the memory—into the rarefied air . . . The dear worries, the sweet troubles of dailiness."

And it has happened. Rita's poem is creating itself—it is a train, she its passenger: "For the first time since I wrote that stupid title down I realized I wrote it down because it had that line about the way to immortality. I realized I was talking about fame."

Naturally, people reading Rita's poem will know none of this. They'll see the poem's themes through the lens of their own ambivalent feelings about whatever are the conflicting demands in their lives. But the tension Rita feels between the satisfactions of fame and accomplishment and the joys of everyday life is her particular lens—and the emotional juice of her poem. Because a new meaning has emerged for that first line written in Rita's sickbed in Germany in 1980, before her life had become a dream ride from earth to the stars: "I want 'em both."

"It's just that I've felt lonely."

"Where's my life? I want a life."

*March 19, 4:30 p.m.*

It comes quickly. Yesterday, the Brandenburg concertos playing for two hours, Rita ripped through four versions of "Sic Itur." Today, the Brandenburg concertos still playing, she whips through five versions. She has found her old musings on melancholy, cribbed an image—"tiny dismissals"—and combined it with the lines on life's trivial irritations from her Mexico notations: "If I close/ my eyes, I'll sink back into/ the day's tiny dismissals." Rita has turned a corner. Forced to work on her poem for *USA Weekend*, impelled to work on "Parlor" at the stable, her mind was somehow freed, her attention distracted momentarily from "Sic Itur," which, inexplicably, allowed Rita to finally see her poem clearly. These so-called distractions cleared a path so that her poem could happen to her, as if she is not the creator of insight, but its recipient. Rita keeps a single quote, in German, tacked to her cabin's bulletin board, the wisdom of Austrian poet Rainer Maria Rilke: *It is not enough for a poet to have memories. You must have very great patience and be able to wait until the memories come again. Memories remain, but the poet changes: You have to wait until it all comes back in a different form to find the meaning.*

Rita is loose now, playing—with words, images, punctuation, enjambment and stanza size. She writes a line, walks out onto it, looks ahead, continues or steps back, tries another. For the first time, she can hear the rhythm of her poem before its words are written, as in a song that doesn't yet have lyrics.

"It's very weird."

She writes:

> Bed, where are you flying to?
> I went to sleep nearly
> an hour ago, and now
> I'm on a porch open

to the stars! If I close
my eyes, I'll sink back into

the day's tiny dismissals—
bagged lunch, the tiny dismissal of a glance—
but no, I'm wide-eyed and barefoot,
catching my death of cold,
nightshirt fluttering white as a sail.

Bed, come back here, I need you!
I don't know my way.
At least leave me my pillow
to remind me what I've rested my dreams on—
my dear/crushed pillow, with its garden of smells.

Rita is suddenly hit with an image that grows from the lines she wrote way back on February 5: "I don't remember a thing,/ not the crease in the sheets."

She writes:

What will they do when they come in
and find me missing, just the shape
of my dreaming creased in the sheets?

The lines make Rita shiver in the way she once shivered when she wrote, "He used to sleep like a glass of water/ held up in the hand of a very young girl." That *feeling*. So much of writing a poem is less like saying a prayer than it is putting together the weekly shopping list. Then comes a sacred moment . . . For Rita, these lines are a fish to keep—a rare poet's epiphany in the muck of craft: "I don't know where it came from. It just came." Then:

Bed, where are you flying to?
I went to sleep nearly
an hour ago, and now
I'm on a porch

open to the stars—barefoot,
catching my death of a cold
in a nightshirt fluttering white

as a sail. Come here, bed,
I need you! I don't know my way.
If I close my eyes, I sink back
into the day's bagged smiles,
the tiny dismissal of a stranger's glance . . .

Oh, what will they do
when they find me missing,
just the shape of my dreaming
creased in the sheets?
Who will tell them what it's like here?
No one else knows but my pillow—

my poor, crushed pillow with its garden of smells!

Then:

Bed, where are you flying to?
I went to sleep
nearly an hour ago,
and now I'm on a porch
open to the stars!

Close my eyes
and I sink back into the day's
tiny dismissals; eyes wide
and I'm barefoot, in a nightshirt
fluttering white as a sail.

Come here, bed,
I need you!
I don't know my way.

What will they say
when they find me missing,
just the shape of my dreaming

creasing the sheets?
At least leave me
my pillow to remind me
what misery I've fled—
my poor, crushed pillow

with its garden of smells!

Out Rita's window, the sun is lingering three inches above the mountains. The days are longer now, but she has been too busy even to notice that it is spring: "Why is spring a she? What gender are the other seasons? Summer is female, surely. And winter, too. Fall? Actually, they're all female." Rita's mind, again, is swirling like water over stones in a stream.

"I had given up on this poem."

"It's a great feeling."

"I'm rolling!"

Rita has deleted the sappy line, "*Lay back. Relax. Gentle landings.*" She has again included "catching my death of cold" but then excised it as too "cutesy-wootsy." "Bagged lunch" has gone in, become "bagged smiles" and gone out: "I don't know what a 'bagged smile' is." She has finally taken out "moonlight cool as peaches," and the cliché "wide-eyed" has become "eyes wide" and will later become simply "open wide." She has added "the tiny dismissal of a glance," which has become "the tiny dismissal of a stranger's glance," a cliché she hates, and which has now become simply "the day's tiny dismissals." She loves the sneering sound of the *hiss* in the word dismissals. The line "Bed, come back here" has become the more direct "Come here, bed."

Remembering her notation to emphasize that this poem should have the feeling of a dream, Rita has added, "I've rested on my dreams," which she hates as a cliché. But she thinks, "Oh, hell, I'm just gonna put the dreams in and see what happens." Working from her epiphanic flash, the lines have become "just the shape/ of my dreaming creased in the sheets," which have now become "just the shape of my dreaming/ creasing the sheets." Rita also has added a stanza space between "just the shape of my dreaming" and "creasing the sheets." That space will force a reader to pause after the word "dreaming," float in the space and ponder the image before moving on to the next line. The newly added gerundive i-n-g ending on the word "dream" also carries action—and the sense that the act of dreaming, not the dream itself, is leaving its impression on the bed of real life. As with her poetry, the product is inseparable from the process. In the words of Yeats: "How can we know the dancer from the dance?"

Rita has added "my dear/ crushed pillow," although she knows it's too corny. She has quickly changed it to "my poor, crushed pillow." Despite the truism that a poet should never use two adjectives when one will do, she wants two adjectives to precede the word pillow. Less for the words than for the double beat of emphasis, which is meant to mimic the intense affection of a child for a blanket, toy or pillow: "It's not always the words themselves that bring you the nostalgia but the sound and the rhythm of the words."

This is Rita's ideal: She wants to take a reader to the place she would go as a girl when she read a poem and suddenly felt her breathing begin to synchronize with the poem's cadence: "Before you know it, your body's rhythm is the rhythm of the poem. That's one of the things poems do. You don't even notice that it's happening. But what convinces you is the way the poem influences your breathing, your heartbeat. It becomes a physical thing."

"You want people to get there."

Rita has realized that the final sentiment of her poem is mundane. After visiting the stars, her traveler discovers the wonder of what she has left behind: "my poor, crushed pillow/ with its garden of smells!"—meaning her ordinary life with Fred and Aviva, the days Rita cooks those quick meals of frozen fish fillets, sliced fried potatoes and salad with Caesar dressing, the evenings they all plop down at the TV and watch Aviva's favorite show, *Star Trek: Voyager*, and then Rita quizzes Aviva for her test on earthquakes and volcanoes, and Aviva is curled up on the chair and in the silence between Rita's questions and Aviva's answers, Rita can hear the sound of the leather creaking as her daughter adjusts her body, which makes Rita think to herself, "There's no sound in the poem. Is there sound in dreams? Sound does funny things in dreams—it's like telepathy."

Of her yearning to travel to the stars and her irritation with daily life, Rita asks herself, "Where you gonna go? Is there anything really better than this?" And how else to be a poet? Aren't the trivial, even irritating distractions of life the wellspring, the clay that makes the pot? A poet free from "the day's tiny dismissals," living only among the stars, will not be a poet for long: "It sounds like the old, corny notion, 'Love will bring you back,' but you know that's what it is. How many different plots do we have in this world? Not many."

For the first time, Rita stops to analyze the poem's rhyme and discovers a surprising array of rhymes, half-rhymes and "cousins" of rhymes: barefoot/nightshirt, my way/they say, creasing/sheets, fled/bed, smells/dismissals, sail/smell. Although a reader wouldn't consciously notice the rhymes, they still weave the poem together, like the reprising melodies of a minuet.

"Okay, I'm ready!"

Rita has been writing versions of "Sic Itur" with different stanza configurations—experimenting, seeing if stanza breaks at different lines carry meanings she hasn't recognized, in the same way that playing with a poem's enjambment can reveal a new insight. But now she realizes how she wants the stanzas constructed: "It's really, really picky." But if "Sic Itur" is a journey up to the stars and back down to earth, it demands a narrow, vertical silhouette on the page: "To lift you up in the sky." And if it is to evoke the simplicity of childhood, it also must look clean and pure on the page. The idea is to reach people not only through words, ideas, images, sounds, rhythms and rhymes, but also through the pattern of ink their eyes see on the page.

She goes through tightening lines to narrow the poem's width and extend its height. Then she adjusts the number of lines in each stanza. From top to bottom: a 1 1/2-line title, 5-line stanza, 6-line stanza, 6-line stanza, 5-line stanza, 1-line stanza: "It's like a mirror image," which makes the tug of the stars and the pull of the world equal in visual weight on the page.

At 5:24, she writes:

### SIC ITUR AD ASTRA
*Thus is the way to the stars.*

Bed, where are you flying to?
I went to sleep
nearly an hour ago—
and now I'm on a porch
open to the stars!

Close my eyes
and sink back to
day's tiny dismissals;
open wide and I'm
barefoot, in a nightshirt
fluttering white as a sail.

Come here, bed,
I need you!
I don't know my way.
What will they say
when they find me missing,
just the shape of my dreaming

creasing the sheets?
At least leave me
my pillow to remind me
what misery I've fled . . .
my poor, crushed pillow

with its garden of smells!

Rita has a few nits . . .

"I'm dotting the i's."

She worries about the word "fluttering" in the line "fluttering white as a sail." Is it necessary? Does it add enough for the space it takes? Unlike prose, which Rita compares to walking through the woods and describing everything you see, poetry is like walking through the woods, coming upon an old, deep well and describing only what you see as you stare down its casing. Poetry is a narrow world made wide. So every word, every line in a poem must stand on its own. But without the word "fluttering," the line is lame: "white as a sail." Pick any line: "just the shape of my dreaming" or "and sink back to." Each adds something—action, an image, lyricism, intrigue, an idea. But wait . . . that one line: "At least leave me." What does it add? Nothing: "It just sits there." "This line and I are going to battle."

Rita's not sure about those three i-n-gs in a row—missing, dreaming, creasing. And she's not sure about the line "Close my eyes"—she might add a comma. Today, she's not even sure about the title—maybe she should go back to "Sweet Dreams," which now carries a touch of irony. But adding "Sweet Dreams" would put too much type at the top of the poem and muck up her mirror-image construction of the stanzas. And for the poem to make sense she still needs the Latin and its translation—"Thus is the way to the stars." Come to think of it, maybe she should go back to translating "thus" as "such"—"Such is the way to the stars." Less pedantic. And she'd better look up the quotation. Turns out to be from Virgil's "Aeneid," which she didn't know: "Oh, shame!" She must attribute it. No room for "Sweet Dreams" now.

Maybe she should move down "Come here, bed, I need you" and move up "just the shape of my dreaming creasing the sheets" so the poem's character flies from sky to earth, earth to sky, sky to earth—a trip that ends back home, where Rita has realized she wants to be. But then she'd lose the spatial pause between "just the shape of my dreaming" and "creasing the sheets." And that word "misery"! Rita wants it to be self-mocking. "What misery I've fled . . ." is supposed to mean that her daily life wasn't misery at all. But the word is too strong. "I think there's a different word that won't ring as many bells. One word. And it should be three syllables, but it might end up having to be two."

*March 26, 1:43 a.m.*
After allowing herself a week of distractions, a week for her poem to simmer, Rita writes:

### SIC ITUR AD ASTRA
*Thus is the way to the stars.*
— Virgil

Bed, where are you flying to?
I went to sleep
nearly an hour ago,
and now I'm on a porch
open to the stars!

Close my eyes
and sink back to
day's tiny dismissals;
open wide and I'm
barefoot, nightshirt
fluttering white as a sail.

What will they say
when they find me
missing—just
the shape of my dreaming
creasing the sheets?
Come here, bed,

I need you! I don't know my way.
At least leave my pillow
behind to remind me
what affliction I've fled—
my poor, crushed pillow

with its garden of smells!

"A poem is never done. You just let it go."

In her cabin, Rita hears the distant woof of a dog. Outside the open window is a faint wind: "The sound of air moving—not quite a breeze, but a sighing—all that the word *zephyr* implies." She remembers a time as a girl when her father said that word. At a gas station, as the attendant filled his tank, her father stood and stretched, faced off into the horizon and said as naturally as if he were asking for the time, "What a lovely zephyr today." Young Rita never forgot the baffled look on the attendant's face.

Where are those few words she jotted?

Ah, here they are:

> Meek, this fallen leaf
> reminds me of a word
> my father used to say—
> zephyr, tilting back to
> gaze up under his brimmed fedora
> as if to coax the air along
> his brow: "What a lovely zephyr
> today." And the gas station
> attendant scratched himself,
> instantly ashamed

And once again, Rita steps out onto the lines . . .

# THE MYSTERY OF GOODNESS

Most Harvard grads go for the bucks and the prestige jobs. Bryan Stevenson is happy pulling down $24,000 trying to rescue convicted men and women from the death penalty. What makes Bryan go? "I feel the pleasure of God," he says.

On the threshing-floor, in the center of the crying, singing saints, John lay astonished beneath the power of the Lord.
— From *Go Tell It on the Mountain* by
James Baldwin

I am not an expert on religion, far from it. But somewhere along the way, I learned that in ancient Jewish legend there is told the story of the lamedvovniks, the 36 Righteous Men who were sent by God to live and work among us, always poor, unnoticed and without glory, unaware of their own perfection. If a Righteous Man were ever discovered, various versions of the legend went, he would deny his identity, disappear and reappear, unknown and unknowing, in a distant place. I do not believe in lamedvovniks. I do not even believe in God. But over the years, I've sometimes puzzled at the idea of these Righteous Men living secretly among us, been reminded that what it means to be truly good was as mysterious to those who lived a thousand years ago as it is to us, with all our modern sophistication.

Lately, after meeting Bryan Stevenson, I've found myself puzzling over these questions once again. But then, that often happens to people after they meet Bryan Stevenson.

This morning, Bryan—31, a lawyer and a Black man—is on the road out of Montgomery, Ala., where he lives, headed for Phenix City, a tiny Alabama town where Bryan's Black client George Daniel has been locked in the Russell County jail awaiting his execution for murdering a white policeman. Just yesterday, a federal court over-turned his conviction and ordered that he be given a new trial.

That is what Bryan Stevenson does. He files appeals. He is one of those much-maligned lawyers who supposedly clog the courts with frivolous petitions meant only to postpone deserving men's dates with the electric chair, gas chamber or needle. He is one of the reasons Chief Justice William H. Rehnquist and countless politicians, including President Bush, have called for limits on the number of court reviews for those sentenced to death. He is one of the reasons that, with nearly 2,400 people on death row, only 143 have been executed since the Supreme Court declared the death penalty consti-tutional in 1976. Today, about 75 percent of Americans favor capital punishment, compared with 42 percent in 1966. For the first time, even a majority of Blacks favor capital punishment. So far, this new public thirst for final vengeance has gone largely unquenched.

Bryan Stevenson is one of the reasons.

At the Russell County jail, Bryan is ushered into a small room where George Daniel is waiting. As Bryan tells him that he'll have a new trial—which might literally save George's life—the thin, 34-year-old man smiles blankly, squeezes his nose tightly, rocks his body gently and bounces his legs to some rapid, internal rhythm. He wears a white jail uniform that is filthy at the crotch. The last time Bryan visited George, his cell was dirty with his own urine. Court records show that at least once during his incarceration George Daniel ate his own feces and that he is mildly retarded. "I need ciga-rettes," he says finally. Bryan promises to get cigarettes, and George is led away. As Bryan leaves, a guard stops him at the jail-house gate and says of George Daniel, "I think he's crazy. I really do. That's just my opinion. We have to make him take a shower and change clothes. I think he's crazy. Some people are playin'. I don't think he is."

Outside, past the electric door and the tall wire fence, Bryan says, "George is one of the men America believes is so evil he must be strapped into an electric chair and killed." He doesn't say this harshly or self-righteously. He says it gently, with eerie understatement. "You know, people always ask me how I can defend these 'animals.' I never understand how they can ask that. The criminal justice system is so corrupt, so racist. I wouldn't want George Daniel out fending for himself. He can't. He's ill. But a civilized society does not execute people like him. Rehnquist can restrict legal options for the convicted, because he can't imagine himself or anyone he loves ever being in George Daniel's situation. But how would Rehnquist feel if his son were in George's place?

"In the end, we are too frail to make these decisions."

I met Bryan Stevenson by chance while traveling through the South, which boasts more than half of America's death-row inmates and about 85 percent of its executions since 1977. Right off, Bryan fascinated me. A graduate of Harvard's law school and John F. Kennedy School of Government, he's the director of the Alabama Capital Representation Resource Center, which is involved in some way with most of the 119 death-row inmates in Alabama. He was offered $50,000 to $60,000 a year to take the director's job, one of the center's board members told me, but Bryan said it was too much money. He settled on $18,000—now up to $24,000. In corporate law, he could make five to 10 times that.

Bryan worked seven days a week, still does, often from 8:30 in the morning to 11:30 at night. On Saturdays and Sundays, he knocks off early to do his laundry and maybe catch a movie. These days, he has little time to play his electric piano, compose music, play basketball or attend church, all of which he once did regularly. He hasn't had a vacation in years. Once a voracious reader, Bryan has read three books for pleasure in the last year. He sometimes worries that he doesn't laugh enough anymore.

Simply put, the man was hard to figure. A person didn't need to believe Bryan's cause was noble, or even correct, to be touched and fascinated by his passion. All through the '80s, while most of his Harvard classmates got rich, he defended penniless murderers. His parents—working people from Milton, Del., near Rehoboth

Beach—certainly didn't understand what their son was doing. "Take the money," Bryan's father said, more than once. With all his degrees, Bryan still drove a beat-up Honda Civic. His mother drove a jet-black BMW 325i. She couldn't figure her son either. What had made him so different—from his folks, his classmates, from America, really?

"I've asked him how he does this day in, day out," said William Newman, a Massachusetts lawyer in Alabama who worked with Bryan on a death-row appeal. "It's Bryan. It's who Bryan is. I'm telling you, Bryan is a prince. I bet you won't find one person who doesn't say that. I'm telling you, he's a saint. You can't say that, I know, but he is. That's exactly what he is." Another Massachusetts lawyer, Stewart Eisenberg, also in Alabama working on an appeal, said, "I am extraordinarily impressed with Bryan, but I'm curious about why a Black Harvard Law School graduate who could write his own ticket spends his time earning next to nothing in Klan country on the back roads of the South."

His curiosity was my curiosity. Bryan Stevenson had rejected America's reigning view of success and money, even justice. Perhaps understanding him—America's reverse image—would tell us something about ourselves. So, not yet having the legend of the lamedvovniks in mind, I set about trying to discover what had made Bryan Stevenson so unlike the rest of us.

The road is home to Bryan. He spends more time driving than he does in his apartment, which is furnished with a single folding director's chair, a stool, two end tables, two small ceramic lamps, a television and a mattress and box-spring on the floor. At the office, the phone rings incessantly. Bryan advises about 60 private lawyers who work on Alabama death-row cases pro bono. He handles an additional 24 death-row cases himself. He supervises a staff of five young lawyers who deal with about 30 cases. At the same time, he must raise about $200,000 a year in private or foundation grants to go with the $300,000 the federal government gives to the center. So it is only in his car, now a gray Toyota Corolla, on the back roads of the South, that Bryan has time to himself. He thinks, meditates, sometimes prays.

He is a thin, athletic man, just shy of six feet, a soccer star in high school and college. He wears short, natural hair and a short beard. He wears unstylish clothes and clunky sunglasses. He talks so softly that I must sometimes strain to hear him. He has no discernible accent, strictly Middle American. In phone conversations, prosecutors and defense attorneys who don't know him usually assume he's white. Once, when Bryan suggested that a defense lawyer try to plead his client down from a death sentence charge to life without parole, the lawyer said, "Didn't I tell you? He's a nigger. Can't get a life plea for a nigger in this county."

"I have always felt," Bryan says, as he drives toward Atlanta to visit another death-row client, "that I could just as easily have ended up as one of the men I am defending. I've had friends, cousins who fell into trouble. It could have been me." Bryan says this quietly and deliberately, with little emotion. When he talks about the death penalty, he talks mostly facts and fairness. He talks like a lawyer. Unless asked again and again, he rarely speaks about himself, not even in the little asides through which most people reveal so much. When I later read his words, I will see that he was, more or less, on a soapbox, plunging point by point through his list of horrors about the death penalty. But as I sit next to him, listening, a gentle intimacy in his manner masks his single-minded agenda.

"I could go through the South's prisons and put together five death rows of men not condemned whose crimes were far more vicious," Bryan says. "The people who end up on death row are always poor, often Black. And almost always they had bad lawyers—real estate lawyers who never handled a capital case and who had to be dragged screaming into the courtroom. In one case, the judge actually sent the defense lawyer out to sleep off a drunk.

"Appointed lawyers, paid a maximum of $1,000 in Alabama and several other Southern states, often do almost no work on their cases. It takes 800 hours to do a capital case. The Supreme Court declared it unconstitutional, but prosecutors in the South still keep Blacks off capital juries by giving bogus reasons to strike them. In one rural Alabama county we found potential jurors labeled by the prosecutor as 'strong,' 'medium,' 'weak' and 'Black.'

"Maybe it would help the congressmen who are so hot for the death penalty if they thought of it this way: Imagine a senator is accused of stealing campaign funds and he is told that he gets a lawyer who's a drunk, who's being paid $1,000. Then the senator is told, if he's a Democrat, that only Republicans will sit on his jury— just as Blacks are still tried by all-white juries. That's our system of justice today.

"Why do I do what I do? How can anyone do anything else?"

Bryan Stevenson was always different. In rural southern Delaware, he was the only Black child in his first-grade class in 1965. His mother, who migrated from Philadelphia through marriage to Bryan's father, had volunteered to put Bryan and his older brother in the white school even before formal integration was in place. She had only to look at the ramshackle schoolhouse Black children attended to know where her kids were going. Years later, when Bryan was put in a slow-learner class with the Black children who had arrived with integration, it was Bryan's mother who went to the school and raised hell until he was bumped to the top class.

Alice Stevenson was a firebrand by the yardstick of southern Delaware. "Don't be a fool, don't be silly and grin," she'd tell her two sons and daughter. "You are here to make a mark. Otherwise you will be the mark." Appalled at the docility she perceived in southern Delaware's Blacks, she admonished her children never to show false deference to whites. She insisted on perfect grammar, diction and pronunciation. And there was one absolute rule: "I never want to hear that you can't do something because you're Black. You can do anything you want."

Bryan's father, Howard, a native of southern Delaware, gave less assertive advice. The child of a prominent Black mechanic in nearby Georgetown, he had grown up playing with the children of the town's prominent whites. He recalls few incidents in which he was mistreated by whites. In fact, because he dressed nattily—refusing to wear the jeans and overalls then worn by most of the Blacks he knew—it was more often Blacks who insulted him with the charge that he was highfalutin. Howard's advice to his children—born of his own unusual experience—was that most white people will treat you well if you treat them well.

Between the two of them, Howard and Alice Stevenson sent a singular message: Whites were not to be feared.

Both had good jobs. She was an accounting clerk at the Air Force base in Dover, and he was a lab technician at the General Foods plant. They bought three acres on County Route 319 and built a little ranch house that was elegant by local Black standards of the day. Up the road, their neighbors lived with dirt floors and no running water. In a sense, the Stevensons were local Black gentry.

Alice worried about her children being in school all day with whites, worried they'd be picked on, worried they'd forget they were Black. In high school, where Bryan was popular, she worried about the white girls who kept calling the house. "Please don't marry a white girl just to do it," Bryan's mother pleaded. Today, she says, "I didn't order him, but I did beg." On the other hand, Alice worried too about her children hanging around with too many Black kids who said "mens" for "men" or who said "I be fixin' to go home now."

But most importantly, she worried about a more profound influence. Howard was a deeply religious man with a Pentecostal bent to his faith. Alice had realized this near the time of their wedding while they were attending a service at her white-gloved Black Baptist church in Philadelphia. Out of the blue, Howard was struck by the power of the Holy Spirit. In the words of the Pentecostals, he "got happy"—and he stood and danced wildly in unconscious, joyful exultation. The ushers came to restrain him. The fiercely proud, urbane and proper Alice was mortified. And back in Delaware at Howard's Prospect AME Church, it was more of the same. To Alice, the congregation's emotionalism was ignorant and hickish. It did not fit with her plans for her children.

The Stevenson kids all did well, went to college and graduate school. But Bryan was always the family's darling. Howard Jr., the oldest, came to resent his father's strict discipline. Christy, the youngest, used to sneak off to listen to rock music. But Bryan—as far as anyone knows—did none of these things. Not to say he was perfect: He picked on his sister sometimes, fought with his brother, bent a few of his father's strict rules. But all in all he was about as good as kids come. A self-taught musician, he played organ and piano at the Prospect AME Church and learned to shift his tempo to the spontaneous outbursts of congregants as they, like his father, "got happy." He showed no interest in being a minister, but he could preach up a storm.

In his overwhelmingly white high school, Bryan was president of the student council. He was a star athlete. He was a straight-A student who would eventually graduate No. 1 in his class. He would be pursued by Ivy League schools but take a soccer scholarship to Eastern College, a small Baptist school in Pennsylvania, where he would lead the gospel choir and a Christian fellowship. In high school, he was a champion public speaker, and he played the lead in "A Raisin in the Sun." After 30 years of teaching drama, Harriett Jeglum still remembers it as the play of which she is the proudest. At Cape Henlopen High, Bryan held an odd status. He was one of only a handful of Blacks in the advanced classes, and it was common for Black kids in that situation to be teased, even harassed by other Black kids—accused of "trying to be white." Bryan's sister, Christy, got some of that grief, but she and her brother and other old acquaintances of Bryan's say he never did.

"He was just so kind and decent," says Kevin Hopkins, a childhood neighbor of Bryan's. "Nobody would ever have thought of saying anything like that about Bryan, Black or white."

Bryan's mother tells this story: When the kids were young, she always told them they could make requests for their favorite meals and she'd do what she could to fix them. Christy and Howard made requests, but Bryan never did. "He just ate whatever I cooked and said it was the best food he'd ever eaten," she says, still sounding a bit puzzled. "That's just the way he was about everything. If I was in a bad mood, he was always the first to notice it. He'd say, 'You all right, Mom?' "

Back on the road to Georgia's death row: "I had the happiest childhood," says Bryan, finally loosened up and talking about himself for a change. "I was at church two, three nights a week, all day on

Sundays," he says. "At school, I knew everybody—the white kids from class, the Black kids from sports. But we lived in the country, and I didn't hang with any clique. My parents cared about me and I wanted to do things to make them care about me more. Years later, at Harvard, so many kids I met felt that if they hadn't gone to Andover and Harvard, their lives would be over." He smiles. "But I always figured that people with even zillions of dollars couldn't be happier than me.

"I had fights with the white kids on the bus. They'd call me 'nigger.' In first grade, I remember holding my hand up and never being called on. In second grade, a teacher's aide made me get off the monkey bars while the white kids were on it. When they did integrate the schools, all the Black kids were in 3-C. I was the only Black kid in section A until junior high. Year after year, the counselors tried to get me to take vo-tech: 'Everybody needs to know how to make bricks,' they said." Finally, as Bryan talks, it becomes clear that the racism he has experienced, mild by the standards of the generation before him, is still tightly woven into his work against the death penalty.

"The reason I always say I've never met a client whose life isn't worth saving," he says, "is because they are like me—except they didn't get in 3-A. They were in 3-C. A few breaks the other way, and I could be on the other side of the table. You know, as a kid, I spent my summers at my aunt's in Philly. You couldn't get police to come to her neighborhood. You had to call and say a police officer had been shot. My grandfather was murdered, stabbed dozens of times, in his own home. The killers pleaded to a low charge. I had a Black friend raped on campus, but the case was never pursued. She was leaving town, had no family there to pressure the prosecutor. That's our justice: We overprosecute crimes against whites and underprosecute crimes against Blacks, because whites have political power and Blacks don't. I saw it in my own life long before I studied the death penalty.

"But when I did, and discovered that a man who murders a white has a 4.3 times greater chance of getting the death penalty in Georgia, I saw it as a symbol of all the race and poverty bias in our society. We're not yet capable of valuing the life of a Black mother of four in the projects the same way we value the life of, say, the ex-president of Chevron. We're just not capable.

"Do you know that in Montgomery, Alabama, there's a paper called the *Bulletin Board* that still runs ads seeking white renters? I spent weeks looking for an apartment. On the phone, a man said, 'You don't sound Black, but I ask everyone.' I lost all humility. I told one woman I was a lawyer with a Harvard degree. She said the apartment was $250. I put on a suit, but when she saw me her whole body sagged. She said the rent was $450. It's very demoralizing and debilitating. None of my Harvard degrees, my suits, meant anything next to my little Black face.

"All these things are of the same cloth."

At the Georgia Diagnostic and Classification Center, which houses that state's death row, Bryan's client, Roger Collins, is waiting in the visitors' room, a deep narrow place with a wall of screened bars and a long row of empty stools. After four years of handling his case, Bryan has come to think of Roger as a friend. Roger stands to greet him, takes away his sunglasses and puts them on, hams it up. He is a Black man and Bryan's age exactly, 31, handsome, with short hair and a close-cut beard. He is on death row for brutally murdering a Black woman 13 years ago. Roger was 18. His accomplice was 25. They had separate trials. Roger got death. His accomplice got life. Roger could get an execution date any day.

Bryan tells him about his appeal and about how Congress might pass a law that would help his case. (As it turned out, Congress did not.) "I understood right from wrong," Roger says. "I did, yeah. It just started out one thing and ended up another. I've done some hellful things in my past." When he was 13, Roger says, he and his father and brother would go to Florida from Georgia and rob places every weekend. In ninth grade, he still couldn't read. He thinks, but isn't sure, that his mother and brother are in prison. His father, who eventually went to prison for murder, is out now, and he visited a few weeks ago. "He said they went for the death sentence," Roger says, "and missed."

"It looks real good," Bryan says. "Don't get down."

Roger says, almost to himself, "Ain't set no date."

Outside, on the road again, Bryan says, "I meet people like Roger every day. Their lives are a mess. Half of my clients have had somebody in their families murdered. They are always getting their electric turned off, or their telephone. Or they mention that their daughter has been in jail for six months, and, by the way, what should they do about it? They live at the margins of society, with no sense of control over their lives. We've given up trying to help them. To mention it is to be ridiculed as naive and weak. You know, as a boy George Daniel was hung in a sheet from a tree when he wet the bed, and beaten with a bat." Bryan is quiet for a long time.

Then he says, "I'm afraid they're going to kill Roger."

Something happens to idealistic young people at Harvard Law School. On the first day, Bryan recalls, his entering class was asked how many planned to practice public interest law after graduation, and probably 70 percent of the hands went up. But very few entered the field. Last year, only about 3 percent of Harvard Law's graduates went directly into legal or public service organizations. In Bryan's class, the overwhelming majority of graduates took prestigious clerkships or cut to the chase and took $70,000-plus jobs with big law firms. "Everybody came into law school wanting to help the poor," Bryan says. "But when the big law firms offered $1,500 a week, they all went."

It was a seduction. On that first day, students were told to look around at their 500 classmates. "They tell you that you're sitting with future congressmen, leading partners of important law firms. You are pushed to compete, get to 'the top.' Only nobody ever stops to define 'the top.' There's no value orientation about finding meaning in what you do." Students are encouraged to feel special, he says, as if they are better than everyone else and therefore deserving of wealth, power and privilege. It can be a very appealing pitch, especially to youngsters from the bottom, who yearn to be accepted by the elite and who are willing to pay the price of distancing themselves from their roots. Bryan didn't bite. It sounds hokey, but Bryan seems instead to have cut a swath of goodness through his years at

Harvard. In the remarks of his former classmates, there is an unmistakable tone of testimony.

"He is just this incredibly exceptional person," says Jeffrey Nussbaum, a lawyer in San Francisco and a former Harvard Law classmate. "Bryan radiated a sense of goodness and kindness, which sounds so mushy. But he definitely radiated it. He has some kind of inner peace." Nussbaum says Bryan was once harassed by a gang of whites in Cambridge. "He wasn't angry. That was the thing. How can I put it? He felt sorry for the people who had attacked him."

Another Harvard classmate, Jerry Salama, now an assistant to one of New York's deputy mayors, even remembers Bryan once talking about his opposition to the death penalty. "What about the guy who cuts people in 50 pieces?" Salama asked pointedly. First, Bryan mentioned that his grandfather had been savagely murdered. Then he said something Salama has never forgotten: "It's not right to kill them back." Says Salama, "He just couldn't fathom the idea of wanting to 'kill them back.'"

Again and again, old Harvard classmates mention that Bryan, who clearly didn't share the law school's dominant values, never criticized anyone for wanting to get rich and powerful by serving the already rich and powerful. "A lot of us were talkin', talkin' all the time about helping the poor, but very few of us did anything about it," says Kimberle Crenshaw, a former Harvard Law classmate and now a UCLA law professor. "Bryan never talked about it. He just did it. He didn't do it to win other people's approval. He did it for himself. He was one of the few people not tainted by Harvard. He's got something else that gives him energy. I don't know what it is. I don't know anybody like him. I think Bryan is religious. I don't know how religious."

Bryan's old classmates mention repeatedly that they "think" Bryan is religious, but they say he never talked about that either. They knew he went to church, but nobody knew where. In fact, Bryan went to church in a poor Black Cambridge neighborhood, where as a volunteer he helped people fight their way through the city's housing and welfare bureaucracies and gave kids free piano lessons.

"Bryan is the kind of person who, even though I don't see much anymore, I will always consider a close friend," says Frederick Smith, a lawyer in New Jersey and a former Harvard Law classmate. "The word for Bryan is seminal. It's hard to be close to him and not be profoundly influenced and deeply changed. I very quickly fell under his wing. Bryan was from a little country town, and I had gone to prep school, Harvard College and spent two years at Oxford, but I had to run to keep up with Bryan, literally." He laughs. "It sounds like I'm talking about someone who is older, but I'm five years older than he is.

"I always assumed that what happened to me would happen to Bryan. 'Well, now's the time to grow up. We have bills to pay.' Everybody else in the class, like lemmings, hopped off the cliff and went to large law firms. But not Bryan. I have another friend from Harvard, and he and I still talk about the phenomenon of Bryan Stevenson. What makes him what he is? We talk about how much we hate what we're doing. Why did we fall so short and Bryan is out there as a beacon? I hate to admit to character flaws, but maybe Bryan is the clearest example of what true character is all about."

Bryan Stevenson doesn't like to hear this kind of talk about himself. It is, he believes, another kind of trap, not unlike the one Harvard lays for its "special" young students. "I know they are trying to be nice," he says, as he drives off to yet another rural Alabama town, this time Monroeville, to talk to the family of his death-row client Walter McMillian. "I hear it when I go to a reunion or I run into an old classmate who's doing something he hates. These people act like I'm a priest, making such sacrifices. I'm not. It's easy for me to do what I do. What people don't understand when they say I could be making all this money is that I couldn't be making all this money. I could not do it. I could not get up in the morning and go to work. If the death penalty were abolished tomorrow, I wouldn't be a corporate lawyer. I'd probably be a musician. When people say I'm great, what I'm doing is great, they aren't talking about me. They're talking about themselves, about what's missing in their lives."

Bryan has struggled with the idea that he is special, denied it, all his life. "Whites have always treated Bryan like he walked on water," says his brother, Howard Jr., a psychologist and visiting professor at the University of Pennsylvania. "But the label of specialness is impossible to swallow, because to be Black and special to whites means you aren't really Black, which puts a distance between you and your people, who are to whites very unspecial. To accept the label of special is to absolve people of their responsibility to be good. It's a different kind of control. It's the desire to take what you have and make it their own."

As Bryan cruises toward Monroeville, past cotton and cane and giant pecan trees, past Alabama's Holman Prison and its death row, I recall for the first time the legend of the lamedvovniks, the Righteous Men, who forever deny their own virtue. Bryan would understand why ancient legend required good men to deny their goodness: To believe you are good, special, better than the rest, is to be neither good nor special.

Finally, I ask, "How important is your faith?"

"It's very important," Bryan says. He explains that in the 1970s he was involved in the charismatic Christian movement. It was a modern version of the backwoods Pentecostalism—with its emotional and sublime encounters with the Holy Spirit—that Bryan's father had practiced all his life. In the 1960s, the faith burst forth and profoundly changed America's stodgy and ritualized mainline denominations. Yet, traditionally, Pentecostalism was a faith of the dispossessed—the poor and the uprooted, from white Appalachia to Black Los Angeles. And Bryan knows this.

"Church is not so important to me today," he says, "but I still glory in the charisma and spontaneity of the Black church, still love to play the piano for a person who stands and dances to the Spirit. It is restorative. A grandmother who stands up and says, 'I've lost my son and daughter in the fire, all my belongings, but I'm here with my grandson and we're gonna make it'—it is more restorative than praying with people who are thankful for their wealth. I must return to that well. If there's an afterlife, that's who it's for—those whose lives have been hellish and who've struggled to be better. That's who

Christianity is for—the rejected, despised and broken. And those are my clients."

It's dark when Bryan arrives in Monroeville and meets Walter McMillian's sister, niece, and nephew in the cold wind outside the IGA food market at Ollie's Corner. He tells them an appeals court has ordered the local court to consider whether the county prosecutor had secret deals with the two main witnesses against McMillian, a 49-year-old Black man who was convicted of killing an 18-year-old white woman in cold blood during a robbery. One witness against McMillian was his alleged accomplice, who pleaded guilty to the murder and got a life sentence. In many of Bryan's cases, it's clear that his clients actually did murder someone. But the evidence against McMillian is strictly circumstantial. If Bryan can prove the secret deals, Walter McMillian gets a new trial.

"Is everything else going all right?" Bryan asks.

"Did my daughter call you?" McMillian's sister asks.

"From Mobile, yes. I haven't had a chance to call back."

"They got her son for capital murder."

"Is that right?" Bryan says, masking his shock with studied calmness. "Have her call me. Make sure she tells him not to say anything to the police. Does he have an attorney?"

"No."

"Make sure she calls tonight."

"How late?"

"Anytime, anytime."

Back on the road, Bryan says, "It's probably too late."

As always, Bryan worries first about the man accused, but right now I can't help thinking about the victim, for whom it is already too late. And I ask the question that is unavoidable, the one so many people believe challenges Bryan's entire work: "But what about the victims, the people your men kill? What about their husbands and wives, their kids? Don't these murderers deserve to die?"

Bryan is silent for a long moment. He has, of course, heard the question many times before. "I feel worse for the families than I do my clients. It's the hardest thing." He is silent again. "But I tell them,

'I don't care what you did, how awful it was. I'm here to get you off. I don't believe you should be killed.' "

"It's not right to kill them back?" I ask.

"It's not right to kill them back," he answers.

By now it's late, nearly 11, and on the drive back to Montgomery I close my eyes, very tired. But Bryan is wide awake, ready to go back to the office tonight to work on several briefs and to meet with Amnesty International representatives who are in town visiting his center. The schedule is grueling, and Bryan does sometimes yearn for regular hours, a wife, kids. But he finds working with his clients so absorbing that he doesn't think much about what he's missing. Besides, he figures he's still young, with plenty of time for a family later. After a while, when we are nearly back to Montgomery, I ask, "Your parents have never understood why you do this, have they? They think you could be earning gobs of money."

Bryan laughs. "They've come to understand me recently."

The next week, on a beautiful autumn day, I leave Washington and drive to Milton, Del., where Bryan grew up. I find his home, the little white ranch house on County Route 319, and his father, Howard Sr., a short, trim man with dark gray hair and black plastic glasses. He takes me to the Prospect AME Church on Railroad Avenue, past the road signs riddled with bullet holes, past Vern's Used Furniture.

It's a small, not so sturdy, white clapboard church about the size of some living rooms I've seen. The sanctuary is adorned with bright flowers, a cloth rendering of *The Last Supper* and a piano and an organ, much like the ones Bryan once played here on two, three nights a week and all day on Sundays. The church, with its vaguely musty aroma, is the very image of the tiny churches that dot rural America, particularly in the South, the very image of the backwoods church that embarrassed Bryan's mother when she first moved to Milton decades ago.

It's a long way from Prospect AME to Harvard Law School, but somehow Bryan made the distance look short and easy. I am marveling at this when I notice that Bryan's father is standing before the little altar, framed by the bright flowers and the cloth rendering of *The Last Supper*, lost in thought. He shakes his head, looks around at the empty sanctuary and says wistfully, "Bryan used to set me on fire when he prayed out loud." And once again I am reminded of how often Bryan's behavior—in childhood, in law school, still today—evokes inspiration in those around him, even his own father.

Back at the house, I see that Bryan's old room is filled with storage boxes now, but that the walls are still papered with dozens of his awards from childhood: the Golden Scroll for the Promise of Greatness, the Thespian Society Award, awards for music, sports, student council—you name it, the guy won it. His parents' pride is not disguised, and the dark-paneled walls of the house are covered with photographs of Bryan, Howard Jr. and Christy.

"Bryan said you only recently came to understand him," I say. "What did he mean by that?"

Without hesitation, Howard jumps up from the couch and dashes to the television. He roots around in a cabinet full of video-tapes and pops one in the VCR. "This was last April," he says. "Bryan spoke to the national youth conference of the AME Church." In a few moments Bryan, all grainy, comes on the screen. And for half an hour, he speaks, starting slowly and then, moved by the power of his own emotions, quickly, like rapids. He says we execute the retarded, the young and the mentally ill. He says we execute men for killing whites far more often than we do for killing Blacks. He talks of the defense lawyer who was drunk and of the Blacks who are so often struck from murder juries. He talks of the judge who said of a convicted man's parents, "Since the niggers are here, maybe we can go ahead with the sentencing phase."

Then Bryan says, "It's not enough to see and deal with these things from a humanistic perspective. You've got to have a spiritual commitment. So many talk that talk, but they don't walk that walk. We've got to be prepared to pay the cost of what it means to save our souls." Then he quotes the Bible—Matthew 25:34-45: "Then the King will say to those at his right hand, 'Come, O blessed of my Father, inherit the kingdom prepared for you from the foundation of the world, for I was hungry and you gave me food; I was thirsty and you gave me drink; I was a stranger and you welcomed me; I was naked and you clothed me; I was sick and you visited me; I was in prison and you came to me . . . Truly, I say to you, as you did it to one of the least of these my brethren, you did it to me.' "

The place is bedlam. "I wouldn't exchange what I'm doing for anything," Bryan says, voice rising. "I feel the pleasure of God."

Bryan's father gets up quietly, rewinds the tape. Tears are in his eyes. "I didn't understand his faith until this talk," he says. "He never talked about himself, ever."

Sadly, Bryan's mother, Alice, is in the hospital being treated for a life-threatening illness, and his father and I go to visit. Her lean, elegant body and handsome face are the image of her son, as are her slow, deliberate mannerisms, perfect diction and clear, accentless voice. She sits in a robe in a chair next to her bed, illuminated by a single lamp. Seeming tired, she closes her eyes as she speaks. "I told him he was not going to live in the sticks all his life. Please do not be satisfied." She opens her eyes and laughs. "Sometimes I think he listened too well. He is so far away. I miss him so. Did Howard tell you we didn't understand him until April of this year when we heard him speak? He never talked about himself. Me, I've been a money-grubber all my life. But now that I've been sick, I see that Bryan is right. Really, what are we here for? We're here to help one another. That's it." After a pause, she says, "You know, a college friend of Bryan's once asked me, quite seriously, 'Could Bryan be an angel?' "

Alice and Howard Stevenson talk into the evening, and just as I'm about to leave, Howard says, "The Lord touched him." And Alice tells this story: When Bryan was 13, in a hot little Pentecostal church in Camden, Del., where she'd taken the Prospect youth choir to sing, "Bryan went off in the Spirit. He got happy. He danced." I ask what that means, and Alice and Howard chuckle at my naiveté. "It is to be in a realm of complete and absolute joy," Alice says, although that day she did not feel joy. "I cried because I never wanted that to happen to Bryan. I didn't want him to be a backwoods cultist Christian. He broke out in a sweat, completely physically immersed, and the Spirit took him over. I held him, hugged him and cried." Because for all the years Alice—proud, urbane Alice from her white-gloved Philadelphia

Baptist church—had gone to Prospect AME, she'd never been a true Pentecostal believer.

"But this was my child, my darling, my flesh. I knew there was no falseness in him. So I knew this was a real gift from God. I stopped turning my nose up at it as something only ignorant people did." And looking out the window one morning soon afterward, watching the rising sun, Alice was suddenly overwhelmed with the presence of God. Simply put, Bryan had saved his mother.

"That feeling," she says, "can't be put into words."

Perhaps not, but I remember that James Baldwin seems to have come very close in the final pages of *Go Tell It on the Mountain*. And rereading his words at my home late that night, I try to imagine Bryan as Baldwin's character John, try to imagine how transforming must have been Bryan's experience—whether spiritual or psychological.

Baldwin wrote: "And something moved in John's body which was not John. He was invaded, set at naught, possessed. This power had struck John, in the head or in the heart . . . The center of the whole earth shifted, making of space a sheer void and a mockery of order, and balance, and time. Nothing remained: all was swallowed up in chaos . . . His Aunt Florence came and took him in her arms . . .

" 'You fight the good fight,' she said, 'you hear? Don't you get weary, and don't you get scared. Because I know the Lord's done laid His hands on you.'

" 'Yes,' he said, weeping, 'yes. I'm going to serve the Lord.' "

I put down the book and I think again of the 36 Righteous Men: The ancient legend, I now realize, isn't the answer to what it means to be truly good; it is only one more way of asking the question. With or without religion, maybe that's all good people can ever really do: live their lives as a question posed to others. I think of a priest I once knew. He told me that Christians would have no need to evangelize if only they lived their lives as mirrors of goodness in which others could glimpse the goodness of Christ—and thus the goodness in themselves. And I think of Bryan: His deepest mission, I now see, is not to save the lives of convicted men, but to live in such a way that his own life is a question posed to others.

"I want to be a witness for hope and decency and commitment," Bryan had said, before I understood what he meant. "I want to show in myself the qualities I want to see in others." Bryan's own motive is to "feel the pleasure of God." Yet whether graced with the power of God, the power of a strong, decent family or the power of some buried psychological zeal, Bryan's life is like the priest's mirror: Looking into him, people see their failings and possibilities. Like the lamedvovniks, Bryan must deny this power—not because he will disappear in a flash of God's will, but because if others can call him "special," they can excuse their failings and avoid struggling to find the goodness in themselves.

Finally, I think of Frederick Smith, Bryan's friend from Harvard Law, the man who said he was forever changed by meeting Bryan: "If religion created Bryan Stevenson," he had said, "we all need a lot more religion."

Pray it were only that easy.

# THE REVEREND COMES HOME

For the Reverend James A. Holman, life has come full circle. In a sermon he once preached, he said, "Some people marry their cross. Some people give birth to their cross. And some people put their cross in a nursing home." So when their once-powerful father became too ill to care for himself, his daughters could see only one choice.

Georgia had never seen her father naked.

Certainly not when he was young and prideful, walking with a bantam swagger that she and her sisters called "the strut"—a walk at once jaunty and commanding, with an unforgiving posture softened by a long, friendly gait and made theatrical by arms that pumped confidently from rolling shoulders. Make a path, folks, here comes the reverend, the Rev. James A. Holman. Georgia's older sister, Leila, when she was a girl, would feign exhaustion just so Daddy would hoist her onto his chest and shoulder, where she'd pretend to be asleep, all the while watching with fascination over his back as his legs, like tiny rockets, launched him and her off the sidewalk with each dancing, prancing step.

That legendary strut, where was it now?

When Georgia first touched his skin in the hospital, helped turn his body in bed or helped change his diaper, she nearly recoiled, as if meeting these intimate needs for her sick 80-year-old father were unnatural acts, a violation of all human hierarchy. She thought to herself: This is not my father.

It was not the father who had mesmerized huge revival crowds with his stunning "Take Up the Cross" sermon. It was not the father who had signed men out of jail on his word alone. It was not the father who had always arrived with pennies for her piggy bank. And, surely, it was not the father who had sat on the front porch rocking her on hot summer nights while he recited poetry.

This frail man's bones poked at his skin like sticks prodding soft leather. This man didn't recognize her, called her "Cat," the nickname for her dead sister, Catherine. This man rambled deliriously about a Rev. Johnson, asked the name of the street where his own former church stood and insisted that one of the nurses was his dead wife, Anna Pearl. This man seemed afraid.

All hours, Georgia and Leila sat beside him, his body as light and fragile as settled dust, his skin dark against the ocean of white sheets into which Georgia was sure he was about to disappear.

She wondered, Where are his dreams taking him tonight?

She wrote in her diary:

"This, the man who held my hand."


But Daddy didn't die . . .

For months, Georgia Kaiser, who is now 50, and Leila Davies, who is now 58, took turns driving or riding the bus back and forth from their homes in Silver Spring and Chevy Chase to Augusta, Ga., where Daddy had left the hospital and was staying with a friend. The commuting was exhausting and expensive. Georgia and Leila were schoolteachers with only so many days off, and they had children and husbands who needed their time.

In theory, they had two choices: Put Daddy in a nursing home or take him into their own homes. But like many elderly people, their father had let it be known that he'd rather die than go into a nursing home. In a sermon Georgia remembered him preaching when she was a girl, he said, "Some people marry their cross. Some people give birth to their cross. And some people put their cross in a nursing home." The sisters really had only one choice.

That was four years ago, just before Georgia cleaned out a room and Daddy moved into her house. When he was strong enough, he began splitting his time between Georgia's and Leila's, only a few miles away. The women's decision to take their father into their homes seemed to Georgia a private choice.

Such private choices will be occurring more and more often in the years to come. By 2025, nearly 20 percent of the population will be 65 or older. In 1900, only an estimated 1 in 10 married couples between the ages of 40 and 60 had two or more parents alive. Today, thanks to a U.S. life expectancy that has risen by about 25 years in the 20th century, more than half of America's middle-age couples are estimated to have two or more parents living.

Despite the myth that modern children dump their parents into nursing homes, only 5 percent of people over 65 are in such facilities, and nearly three-quarters of the nation's frail elderly are cared for by family members who live in the same residence. The numbers are daunting: In 1985, there were about 6.5 million dependent elderly in various living arrangements. By 2020, there will be an estimated 14.3 million. Hardly a family in America will be untouched.

But Georgia Kaiser wasn't thinking about other families. First came her duty to her father. Beyond that she worried how her own life and her own family would be changed. Deep down, she childishly wished her father hadn't gotten feeble. Then she felt guilty for feeling this. As Georgia packed his things for the move to Washington, she stuffed her father's old family photos and memorabilia in a brown box and put it all away, unable even to look. She thought, This is all that's left of him. In her diary, she wrote: "If you should go and I remain, whatever shall I do?"

Looking back now, looking at her family as a human laboratory for what is about to touch so many lives, Georgia believes life with Daddy has turned out to be a bittersweet blessing for her, Leila, their children, their husbands—and for Daddy. Don't get Georgia wrong, it has been no picnic for any of them. But it has been no horror show either. It has made her feel good to know she has returned what was given her as a child, and it has created a time tunnel through which she, her family, even her father have looked back and ahead at their own lives. She puts it simply.

"I feel more grown up."

They are brother relics: the reverend and the curio.

He is 84. The curio—a dark wooden cabinet with a curving glass front, three shelves, feet that are carved into animal paws and a horizontal mirror that rests on a warping top—is probably that old too.

The reverend was only 15, working as a delivery boy at a dry goods store in his hometown of Americus, Ga., when he heard two sisters from the family that owned the store mention that they were selling the curio to make room for a new piece of furniture. The boy spoke up, saying he'd love to buy it as a gift for his mother, and the deal was struck: 50 cents from the boy's $3 weekly wage for 40 weeks—$20, a lot of money in 1925. The boy borrowed a truck and delivered the prize to his mother, who was elated. Sixty-four years passed. And when Georgia was packing her father's books and rolltop desk and a few other belongings, the curio was the only item he asked her to bring along.

"If you can," he said.

The curio and the boy, now antiques.

The reverend sits in a tall, flowered wing chair to the left of his curio. He is a militantly dignified man, his shoulders still erect, his head bald and buffed on top, his remaining hair short and snowy white against his skin. He shaves himself and does a good job, leaving only a few patches of gray beard. His face, like his body, is taut and lean, his cheeks high and hollow, his forehead remarkably unwrinkled. As always, he wears a white shirt and a tie, this day dark blue with a diagonal gray stripe and held in place with a gold tie bar. When he was young, he required two starched and ironed white shirts a day, which Anna Pearl delivered without fail.

He crosses his thin left leg over his right leg at the knee, adjusts his wooden cane against his side, plants his elbows on the chair's armrests and steeples his fingers. He rubs his palms together softly, barely touching, then plays with the change in his pocket. For a moment, he taps his cane with the nail of his finger, then lightly rubs his thigh with his right palm.

He does not squirm, but rather makes each move with a methodical, almost self-conscious elegance. He holds his hands at his chest and rubs them together slowly, as if working lotion into his skin. The hands are large, with long, expressive fingers that seem to curl upward after their middle joints. On the bridge of each hand is a spider web of wrinkles that seems to record his many years like the rings of an old tree. But his palms are as smooth and glassy as pebbles drawn from a running creek. Unlike a laboring man's, his hands were not his most precious tool.

"Let me tell you a story," he always says, his coarse, gravel voice animated by an array of rising and falling volumes and pitches and a masterful range of poetic rhythms, hesitations and inflections. "I was sitting in the house, the telephone rang and it was a young lady whose husband was a Pullman redcap . . ."

This is not the man who moved into Georgia's house four years ago. After what doctors called a "seizure," that man's memory was wrecked and he had to be taught to walk again. That man was so frail and confused, he spent the early days at Georgia's house in bed, not knowing where he was. He constantly apologized for being in the way. At night, he rambled about the house knocking on doors, saying, "Time to go, anybody taking me to work?" One night he got up and packed his bag for a trip he'd gone on years before. He couldn't take himself to the bathroom. He had to be reminded to eat. He had to be told, "Daddy, here's your shirt, put this on." Night after night, he asked, "Where am I?" And Georgia answered, "Daddy, you're with me." And he asked, "Now, who are you?" When Georgia returned from a brief trip, he told her that the man and the girls in the house had been very nice to him.

"Daddy, that's my husband."

"Your husband?"

"Daddy, that's Carl and those are my children."

"Those two girls? Well, they certainly were nice to me."

It was almost more than Georgia could bear. "This is my father!" She couldn't get past her perception that he was now the child, she the parent. She remembered her mother nursing her 93-year-old father. "I'm taking care of Papa," her mother would say. She remembered her father's mother, who lived to be 104, sitting on the porch of the family home in Americus, where she lived with two daughters. She remembered Uncle Willie, crazy with dementia and sick with cancer, who lived with his wife until he finally died. She remembered Uncle Robert, never quite right after returning from World War II, who lived with his sisters for the rest of his life.

Georgia was a grown woman, but she couldn't accept that it was now her turn. "I was in charge of him," she says. "I've got to tell this man what to do . . . This is my father, who would tell me." She balked at the profound gap between saying, "Daddy, dinner's ready," and saying, "Daddy, come eat dinner now."

"I just hadn't grown up to that."

Her father's illness also threw Georgia into renewed mourning for her mother, who had died three years earlier. "It just made a microscopic image of the fact that she's dead, and he's alone . . . All the things that had been, never would be again." Then, in the midst of it all, her father angrily accused her of trying to steal his money. "It hurt me," she says. "I was angry. How dare he!" She sometimes thought: "I wish he were not here. I don't mean dead . . . I don't wish he were in a nursing home. But I wish it hadn't happened. That's what I wish. I wish it hadn't happened."

Georgia even found herself wondering if her enfeebled father wouldn't be better off dead. But each morning, when she went to awaken him, she worried that he might actually be dead. Then it hit her: What if Karen or Lisa finds him dead? From then on, she made sure waking up Grandpa wasn't one of her daughters' chores.

The oddest things irritated her. On the first evening that her father was well enough to eat at the dining room table, he happened to sit in Georgia's chair. "That night I let him," Georgia says. But she was astounded how much his sitting in her chair annoyed her. It was silly, irrational. She knew that. But she couldn't help herself. Then she remembered something her father had told families he counseled as a minister: "People argue about what they're not angry about." Of course. It wasn't the chair: Daddy was here and her life was forever changed. She wasn't angry at him but at her helplessness in the face of it all. After about a week of stewing, Georgia politely said, "Daddy, you're going to sit here now." Daddy did, never knowing the little psychodrama that had unfolded, and Georgia reclaimed her place at the table.

*Summer 1954, Georgia is a little girl* . . . It's hot and dusty in rural north Georgia, in the towns of Gainesville and Dahlonega, before air conditioning, a time of straw hats and cardboard fans, a time when sweaty shirts drew no disapprobation. Little Georgia, with her pretty cotton dress, is the apple of everyone's eye—the Rev. Holman's daughter, the youngest by eight years, spoiled by his undivided attention, the daughter who most takes after his outgoing manner, who, like him, loves books and poetry, a good speaker too, and polite to a fault. When the reverend comes to town on the dirt-road revival circuit, often carrying little Georgia along, the church women pretend to bicker over who'll get her for the day—for sewing or fishing or, just for fun, a stint picking cotton. She is a princess because Daddy is a king.

Every night, Georgia takes her place in the front pew. If Daddy's revival is set to start at 7, it starts at 7, not a minute or 30 minutes after. In a world of dynamic Southern preachers, the Rev. James A. Holman always held his own. He'd graduated from Atlanta's Gammon Theological Seminary and in 58 years of ministering rose to become a presiding elder in the Christian Methodist Episcopal Church. He ran his churches like a benevolent dictator, not only giving the sermon but picking the choir music too. And no chatter in the pews, no droning on about fund-raising picnics. No, Daddy was a choreographer of spiritual emotion. To Georgia, it was as if the whole congregation went into a magical trance, left themselves behind and entered a realm of Daddy's making. He could "line a hymn" like nobody—prayerfully announce or echo each line, turning a hymn into a sermon in itself.

Says Georgia now, "It was a big life."

But three decades later, living in her home, he shuffled along the walls, his hand bracing him as he went. He stuffed bread into his pockets at the dinner table and was terrified to be alone, afraid an intruder would kill him. He picked up schoolbooks, magazines, pens, pencils and hoarded them. He hid soiled and stinking clothing in the corners of his room. When Georgia read him their favorite poem from her childhood, Rosa Hartwick Thorpe's "Curfew Must Not Ring Tonight," he did not recall it.

*Again, Georgia is a girl* . . . It is 1 in the morning and she wakes up instinctively, waiting for her father to return from his weeknight job as a waiter at the Buckhead Elks Club. She hears the door open and close and, as footsteps come down the hall, "Where's my baby?" Then, predictable as dawn, she hears her mother say, "James, don't wake her up." When the bedroom door opens, Georgia feigns sleep until her daddy says, "Here's some pennies I brought you. Put them in your bank and get back in bed."

*Another time* . . . Georgia comes home from junior high school three days in a row and thoughtlessly lets the screen door slam. Each day, her father tells her not to let it slam. After the third day, he stops her and says she's in trouble. Then he makes her go in and out the door five times without slamming the screen.

*Sunday night, suitor night* . . . Georgia's teenage boyfriend comes to the house and sits in the parlor with his beloved and they watch television. At 10 o'clock, Daddy comes in to watch his favorite half-hour of TV, "The Loretta Young Show," and sees the boy give Georgia a little kiss on his way out the door. Daddy says nothing, but the next morning tells Georgia that for a boy to kiss her in her father's home is an act of disrespect. She is not to see the boy again. Every day, Georgia sneaks around the corner and calls the boy on a pay phone. After a week, her father says, "You don't have to call on the phone around there. We've got a phone, and he can come back."

But three decades later, living in Georgia's home, her father didn't always recognize her. She wrote in her diary:

"Not the man that I remember."

Sitting in the tall, flowered wing chair to the left of his curio, the reverend tells his story about the phone call from a young lady whose husband was a Pullman redcap. She asked the reverend to do an anniversary service and he agreed. He says he got down on his knees and asked God for guidance with his sermon. He thought of the Bible story about a man on his way to Jericho who fell among thieves and was left for dead. The man was passed by a priest and a Levite, before a Samaritan took pity on him, bound up his wounds, took him to an inn and paid his way. Jesus said, "Go, and do thou likewise." In this Bible story the reverend found a good message for train porters, who, like the Samaritan, had many chances to do a traveler good. "When I preach," the reverend says, "I aim at something just like I'm shooting at a bird." He says he didn't just preach God is love. He always laid down a challenge, a tough challenge. He pauses, leans forward, cocks his head and smiles.

"I'm sorry if I bored you."

The reverend sits on the edge of the piano bench. In movements so deliberate they seem sculpted, he shifts his cane from his right hand to his left, turns to his right and lowers the arm of the record player onto Frankie Laine's version of "I Believe." Behind him on the chalkboard is printed, "God Is Our Refuge."

At the Holy Cross Hospital Adult Day Care Center, where he and about 30 others go every weekday, the reverend's Tuesday morning prayer meeting is about to begin. The congregants arrive slowly— two in wheelchairs, four with canes, one who is blind, one who is nearly blind, one with her chin bent violently to her chest, one with a gnarled hand, one who bobs her head repeatedly as if responding to a conversation only she can hear, one elegant old woman dressed in a bright green jacket and looking as if she's about to play golf at the country club.

The reverend, still the choreographer of spiritual emotion, intones, "We humbly ask you to give us your attention for these few minutes." His voice is tranquil, soothing, confident. He stands, leans on his cane with his right hand. With his left hand, he gestures in a half moon, his long, dexterous fingers wide and open and seeming to trail behind the sweep of his palm like the spreading tail of a comet. "Whatever else you have to discuss, social matters, jokes, let's forget them now . . . Our theme here is 'God Is Our Refuge' . . . This is a prayer meeting."

An old woman begins to read the 91st Psalm from her Bible, and the reverend gently touches her shoulder and whispers, "Not now," as Frankie Laine sings: "I believe that somewhere in the darkest night, a candle glows . . ." And the reverend, conjuring the magical trance Georgia remembers from childhood, lines the hymn.

"I believe above the storm the smallest prayer . . ."

"Above the storm . . ."

"Will still be heard . . ."

"Do you believe that?"

"Every time I hear a newborn baby cry . . ."

"You believe it . . ."

"Or touch a leaf . . ."

"Touch a leaf . . ."

"Or see the sky . . ."

"That's belief . . ."

"Then I know why, I believe."

"You hear those words? You know why you believe."

The reverend pauses for a long moment. Everyone is silent. One woman has tears in her eyes, two other women hold hands. He switches his cane from his right hand to his left, reaches out and again touches the shoulder of the old woman with her Bible open to the 91st Psalm. He nods to her and says, "Now."

It took about six months after Daddy moved into Georgia's house before she realized she had her father back. After the first few months, he'd begun spending half his time at Leila's, which gave Georgia a respite. His memory was much clearer, he bathed and dressed himself, although even today his clothes must be laid out every morning or he might put on yesterday's dirty clothes. Eventually, he agreed to wear Depends, which made his occasional accidents only a nuisance.

His sharp humor returned and he and Georgia spent many evenings reminiscing, he telling her stories she did not recall and she telling him stories he did not recall. Georgia was once more able to think of those childhood moments with her father—when he made her go in and out the screen door five times or brought her those pennies or banished her boyfriend—without mourning that he was no longer the same man. She took out the brown box filled with her father's old pictures and memorabilia, the box she had put away, and pored over the material, laughing and crying joyful tears as she went.

Because Daddy was the same man, but only in flashes. When he cracked a joke about Georgia's driving: "Too bad the brakes on my side didn't work." When he asked to be taken to Metro's Kiss & Ride so he too could get a kiss. When he got sad after reading that a stray bullet had killed a child. When he put on his black fedora at that certain rakish angle, stopped, glanced back over his shoulder, touched the brim and smiled. When Georgia took a different route to Holy Cross and he asked, "Where are we going?" and she said, "I couldn't lose you, could I?" and he beamed.

"It makes me feel that, yes, family and love and care will make a difference," Georgia says. "He's so much better." And, "I'm definitely a better person. I'm a more tolerant person . . . the change in me that I didn't think I needed to have."

Daddy had always been a hard man to live with. As a minister, he was accustomed to the spotlight, craved and demanded it. Anna Pearl also had spoiled him rotten—not only supplying his starched shirts, but getting up to fetch him a glass of water or a snack whenever he asked. Decades ago, when he smoked Camel cigarettes, no ashtray was ever so close that he wouldn't summon Anna Pearl to move it closer. Once, just after the reverend had left home for a tour of the Holy Land with a group of ministers, she hopped in the car, sped after the bus, beeped her horn and motioned the driver to the roadside: The reverend had forgotten his favorite hat.

But Georgia soon realized that if she had changed her life to accommodate Daddy, he too had changed. For instance, he'd always been a finicky eater. A woman on the revival circuit had once packed him a lunch and later found him down the road feeding it to the hogs. But now Daddy ate everything without complaint. All his life, Daddy had refused to eat garlic, but now he did. All his life, Daddy had refused to eat chicken. Now he did. Leila even believed he'd come to like chicken. Privately, the reverend still detests it. He laughs. "I'm looking to be as easy as I can."

The changes went beyond food. Growing up in the Old South, Daddy always had a deep fear and distrust of white people, but he went to the integrated Holy Cross center and became good friends with many whites, even deferring to one white woman's insistent requests for an occasional peck on the lips. Daddy'd had a temper as a young man, but he had almost no temper now. He'd also had an opinion about everything. So when he arrived, Georgia never yelled at her daughters in front of him, sometimes took them out to the car for scolding, afraid her father would judge her a bad mother. But he never said a critical word about how she and Carl raised the girls, and he never said a bad word about the girls either, only praised them. When Georgia was embarrassed by one daughter's temper tantrum, he said calmly, "We all get angry . . . They're doing fine." Daddy also had always hated cats, but now he loved Georgia's cat, sat petting it, even let it sleep on his bed. In his own way, Georgia realized, her father was trying hard to fit into the family. At his age, over the hill, he was still growing.

Even Carl, who hadn't felt close to Georgia's father and who believed he was too domineering and self-centered, came to admire him. He loved the wise aphorisms the reverend dropped from time to time. Carl's favorite: "Just because you didn't mean to step on my toe, doesn't mean it didn't hurt." Carl had always cooked most of the family meals, and he quickly added softer fare to accommodate the reverend. He cooked the reverend's breakfast and freely pitched in to help Georgia with the new workload. That made life easier for her, but it also had an unexpected benefit: It deepened Georgia's already deep affection for her husband of 21 years.

Georgia's and Leila's greatest fear was what Daddy would do with his time while they and their husbands were at work. Then a neighbor told Georgia about the Holy Cross day care center, which saved the day. Because the reverend's only income was $568 a month in Social Security, he qualified for Medicaid to pay the center's $51-a-day cost. Georgia and Leila worried that Daddy wouldn't go—he had always refused to socialize with old people and was still nervous around whites. But again, he surprised them. He said, "The people there, I could be a morale-builder for them."

Soon, the reverend was center stage at the center, eager to arrive before 8:30 so he could greet everyone in the morning, always inviting one of the women to dip a finger in his coffee to sweeten it up, always asking at the morning gathering, "What's for lunch?" And when he began his Tuesday morning prayer meetings, he was again able to do his life's work. Having people pay attention to him and listen to him, making a contribution again, being accorded special respect and status enlivened him.

The reverend's condition improved, but Georgia still struggled with her grief at her father's decline, still felt ashamed that she wished he didn't need her care, still felt guilty that his presence in the house grated on her. He's not doing anything to bother me, she thought, but he's still getting on my nerves doing it. She began attending the center's group counseling sessions, where she saw that her emotions were downright mundane, as she heard others caring for elderly loved ones gripe about the same kind of irritations. She thought, Hallelujah, somebody feels the same way!

She saw that her burden was neither unique nor the heaviest to bear. At her last session, a man explained that his wife couldn't remember where anything went in the house they'd lived in for 50 years. Another man said his elderly wife had become so incontinent that even with adult diapers, the church choir had finally asked that she retire. A woman said of her stroke-victim husband, "He's like a dummy sitting there . . . I don't know how I do it. It's getting harder and harder."

When the center's director, Bob Grossman, said that as many as half the people over age 85 have some form of dementia, Georgia felt suddenly blessed by the clarity of her father's memory. When he explained that people caring for the elderly often suspect that their charges are pretending frailty to get more attention, Georgia felt relief: She was not an ungrateful daughter, she was only human.

Georgia learned that beyond the confines of the center was a full spectrum of elderly life—elderly people living independently, those living in group homes with special assistance, those living bedridden in relatives' homes with help of professional aides and nurses, those living in nursing homes. The sad truth is, few elderly people die today without some period of dependency. Georgia's father could be in better health, but he also could be in worse health. For that, Georgia was grateful.

And she realized she'd been wrong: She had not become the parent, her father the child. A needful child will become less needful, grow in strength and self-mastery, and a parent burdened with the demands and irritations of constant care knows this, anticipates it. That anticipated future is part of the joy. In Daddy's case, the joy was strictly in the here and now, because the longer he lives the more he will decline. The more jokes he will be unable to finish, the more often he will repeatedly ask Georgia what time a favorite TV show starts, the more often he will hang his dirty clothes in the closet, the more often he will not know what day of the week it is, the more often he will apologize for boring his listeners. But there will be satisfaction later, after his death, in knowing she was a good daughter.

"When I look into his casket," Georgia says, "I want to know my mother is looking here, saying that I did a good job. And I want to be able to say, 'I did a good job.' "

Leila never attended the counseling sessions, and it amazes Georgia that her sister didn't agonize over their father moving in. Leila is a practical-minded, matter-of-fact woman. "We have little things that bother us, but so what?" she says. "This is life." Leila enjoyed hearing Daddy's stories about her childhood. She loved it that her husband, Langston, and Daddy would sit for hours talking about the Bible. She glowed with pride that he always found the strength and concentration to comport himself with dignity at her church's Sunday services, a couple of times even giving a decent sermon or prayer.

Leila took her father's presence in stride, while Georgia struggled with it. Perhaps because Georgia was the youngest by so many years, had been babied and spoiled in that role, had shared a love of books and poetry, she saw more of herself in her father. Who knows? At the counseling sessions, seeing the wide range of people's ways of dealing with their aging parents and spouses, Georgia realized there was no right way to respond.

She says, "It lifted a lot off my shoulders."

Back at his Tuesday morning prayer meeting, the reverend leads in reciting the 23rd Psalm—"The Lord is my shepherd . . ."—and then, his voice strong, his eyes closed, he prays: "Father in heaven . . . here we are now. Our heads are white with the frost of many winters, our faces are wrinkled with the furrows of age and our bodies are bent beneath the weight of years, but in spite of all that, You have sustained us and kept us in the evening of our lives . . ." And the voice of Frankie Laine again rises: "I believe that somewhere in the darkest night . . ."

He is in his room at Georgia's house. It is evening. He often secludes himself here, no phone, no bother. In this room, with a blend of prayer and conversation, he talks to his wife, hears her voice when she says of their daughters, "Stand by them. They're all you have." He reads from the scores of religious books he has collected, searching for themes and passages for his Tuesday prayer meeting. For next week, he selects a stanza of poetry originally written in ancient Sanskrit: "Look to this day, for it is life, the very breath of life."

He sits on his bed, a big bed covered with a brown and white quilt, in a small, darkly paneled room. Around him: a picture of Jesus, a bronze relief of *The Last Supper*, a sepia-toned photo of his father, a handsome man with mustache, white shirt, dark jacket and old-fashioned necktie, a photo of Anna Pearl, his roll-top desk, which is cluttered with pens and pencils, its top drawer holding the false teeth he no longer wears, his last automobile license plate—DDR 207—posted on the wall, two ties already tied hanging from a hanger on a hook near the closet. Everything washed with light turned a vague amber through a tan shade.

The reverend studies and then presses a button on the tape recorder next to him on the bed, inserts a tape, to do what he enjoys so much: listening to his old sermons, some dating back 20 years. When Georgia moved away, she asked him to tape them and send them to her so she could hear them. Now it is he who hears them. Sometimes he gets ready for bed and climbs under the covers to listen. Sometimes he paces the room, gesturing along, moving his lips to his own words. Sometimes he lines the hymns out loud. He thinks of himself as an old preacher listening to a young preacher. He is not that man anymore, but still he is.

"I'm that preacher. I'm doing that speaking now."

"That's me."

"I haven't changed."

"I still have the same philosophy."

"I was"—he hesitates—"good."

"Something that I did that turned out to be magnificent."

"Be that it made some contribution."

The voice on the tape is more than the voice of the Tuesday prayer meeting, layers more. A deep, powerful, chest-rumbling voice, preaching and singing at once, a voice somewhere between that of a whispering prayer-giver and that of a bellowing auctioneer: "Anybody can live good when there ain't nobody botherin' ya! Anybody can live good when they got a good job! Anybody can live good when there ain't nobody pickin' at your wife! Anybody can live good when the money is right!" In that church decades ago, amens and laughter arose.

"But if you stand with God when the chips are down!"

"Everybody! Because it's a cross."

"Jesus, keep me near the cross."

On his bed, a white handkerchief held to his face like a mask, his dark hand silhouetted against it, the reverend cries.

Living with Grandpa has been a complicated ride for his three granddaughters. Leila's son, Paul, was 22 when he arrived, and he took the change in stride. He wasn't home much and eventually married and moved out of his folks' home. But for Leila's daughter, Ursula, then

18, and Georgia's daughters, Karen and Lisa, 15 and 14 at the time, their grandfather's arrival loomed larger. Politeness is an enforced virtue in both families, and the girls were never rude to their grandfather, but inside they often fumed as they struggled to understand his place in their lives.

"I couldn't understand why he was coming all the way here," says Ursula, now 22. "I worried about having to stay home and baby-sit him. I don't mean to sound selfish, but I had my life too. I couldn't understand why they didn't put him in a nursing home nearby and we could go visit him."

It was Ursula's job to clean the downstairs bathroom and it irked her that her grandfather didn't always hit the mark. The idea of sharing the same bathtub with an old man also annoyed her, and she always sanitized the tub before she bathed. He put half-consumed cans of soda back in the fridge. He sometimes used Ursula's drinking cup. He interrupted conversations and told the same jokes and stories repeatedly. He asked, "Ursula, you heard this one?" She answered, "Yes, Granddaddy." Then he told the joke anyway. But worst of all, Ursula was embarrassed for her friends to meet him. He was so, well, so old.

"It was just not cool," Ursula says. "Only in the last year have I started to pay attention to him." She has learned to put away her drinking cup so he won't use it by mistake. She has learned to say, "That's a good one, Granddaddy," when he interrupts with a joke that she has heard before, and then go back to her conversation. She has tried to imagine what it will be like to someday ask her own father, "Daddy, did you go to the bathroom?" before they walk out the door. She has listened to her grandfather tell horrible stories about life for Blacks in the Old South, and she has resolved to complain less and appreciate more the opportunities open to her today. From her grandfather, she has taken this lesson: "Even though he has aches and pains and can be forgetful and had his wife die, he still seems to enjoy life."

Sometimes, Ursula will be in a hurry in the morning, running out the door, trying to get her grandfather off to the day-care center and herself off to Howard University, and he will step outside and say, "Look at the sky, not a cloud! And the grass is so green." That makes Ursula stop in her rush, look at the sky and the grass and see that he is exactly right.

She says, "It's an inspiration."

Karen and Lisa, 19 and 18 today, tell of similar journeys. In the early days, Karen couldn't help but be amused when her grandfather got up in the middle of the night and knocked on doors—it was just so weird! It bugged Lisa that he claimed a chair in the TV room as his own, when nobody had ever had assigned chairs in the TV room. When she sat in it, he shuffled around nearby, hoping she'd get up. But she didn't. Not unless he asked, which he rarely did.

Georgia didn't have as much time for the girls and that bothered them. But once again, it was the trivial irritants that irked them the most. New, unpleasant odors filled the house. Grandpa left the toilet seat up. He tilted lamp shades to read and left them crooked. It angered Karen terribly that she and her sister had to squeeze their chairs on one side of the dinner table. He went up and down the stairs so slowly when Lisa was behind him that she became convinced he did it to annoy her. Both girls believed their grandfather acted more feeble than he was so they'd wait on him—get him a drink, a snack, a newspaper—just as Grandma had always done.

Karen harbored the deepest resentment, which she kept to herself until just last year, when she talked with Georgia about what she had come to see as her irrational anger at her grandfather. "He didn't do anything, really," Karen says. "It was me."

Karen felt gypped. "I wanted grandparents like my friends' who took them shopping and on trips and to a play." She believed her grandfather's infirmity was something he'd done to himself. "I couldn't see that he was just old," she says. Karen also was angered by stories that her grandmother had waited on her grandfather "hand and foot." Unlike her mother, Karen saw nothing quaint in this. She thought, "Why should a woman have to do that?" When her grandfather seemed to expect Karen to do him small favors, she couldn't help but think he was treating her the same way, like a servant. "It disturbed me for so long," she says. "I didn't know the context."

"Looking back, I just wasn't at all compassionate . . . Now I realize he didn't like being so dependent. That's something I've thought about: What if I couldn't do anything by myself? I wouldn't feel good about it, and I'm sure he didn't either. What if I were paralyzed in a car accident? I realized that's how he must feel."

Last year, Karen began to sit in the yard and talk with her grandfather. Without being asked, she did his laundry occasionally and was surprised at how the smell of his soiled clothing no longer sickened her. She found herself listening intently as her mother and grandfather told old stories on each other and found herself imagining her own children and grandchildren someday sitting with her, an old woman, talking about the life she was living right now.

And she saw herself in their stories, realized that her grandfather had seemed to act so strict when her mother was a girl but was actually quite indulgent—a carbon copy of how Georgia had raised her and her sister.

"We're all pretty much alike, as much as I'd like to think I'm different," Karen says. "But pretty much I'm not." Lisa's resentment of her grandfather was never as deep as Karen's, and she says only that she has learned patience from living with him. But Karen's silent anger was once so fierce that she still sometimes asks God to forgive her for it. She has had long talks with the man she dates about how when her parents get old, she will expect to take them into her home. Like her cousin Ursula, when her grandfather moved in, Karen couldn't understand why they didn't just put him in a nursing home. Now Karen understands. "I knew it would hurt him to know we put him out . . . I also wouldn't want him to think I was the kind of person to put him out.

"I'm glad I grew up."

His room at Leila's house is larger and brighter, though it is still cluttered with his books. He sits on a stiff-backed chair, stiff-backed himself, rubs the palm of one hand lightly along his thigh and with his other hand plays with the change in his pants pocket. A person has to understand: The feeling the reverend got while preaching was the most powerful emotion of his life. More powerful even than his love of his wife or his children. That's why listening to his old sermons and conducting his prayer meeting at the center mean so much to him. They touch the old emotion—the power, the joy, the intimacy with God—that he felt every Sunday and every revival for half a century. Like an aging athlete who still feels as if he should be able to make the mark but cannot get his body to cooperate, the reverend still feels like a young man, although his mind and body won't cooperate.

"I feel like I have something to offer . . . I'm afraid people don't want to hear it . . . It's difficult for me to come to that place, but the only way not to come to that place is to die . . . You adjust. You wake up on Sunday morning and say, 'Now if I was in Americus, I would have a place to preach this morning.' I don't have a place. So I put on my clothes and go to church."

The reverend, in his deliberate way, brushing his face lightly with one hand, tapping his cane with the nail of a finger, says it has been a joy to live with his daughters and their families, seeing his grandkids grow up, seeing how competent his daughters are as mothers and wives, seeing how decent are their husbands. "I had a wife who was almost a mother to me," he says. "I was known as a spoiled brat." But as an old man, living with his daughters, he has learned something about compromise, about not always getting his own way. It may have been a long time coming, but the reverend says, "I learned how to get along with people." He acknowledges that, yes, he does make little demands on his family just to get attention. He asks for juice or cookies, asks someone to recite a poem or listen to him recite a poem. "I just abhor loneliness," he says. "I do like babies, I cry." He smiles. "I need attention. I need to feel like they need me."

When the reverend was a young minister, he would go to the home of an elderly preacher he knew to help him bathe, make sure he got a haircut when he needed it. He ran errands, picked up the old man's spending money at the bank. "That man had something to offer," the reverend says, "but he needed help to do it." Once again, he tells the entire story of his sermon in honor of the Pullman redcap, which reminded the baggage handlers that they had many chances to do a traveler good. The message: "Everyone can make a contribution."

At Holy Cross, the reverend knows elderly men who say little, are perhaps locked in their loneliness or debilitations. So he talks to them, compliments them, because he believes he knows what they want and need—attention. Because if a person doesn't get attention, it's as if he has disappeared.

"The ones I ask," the reverend says of Georgia and Leila, "are the ones I gave glasses of water to when they couldn't get them. Reciprocity is the order of the day . . . I feel like my daughters are obligated . . . I need it done and I feel like they ought to know I need it done." It's harder to get up and get a drink, he says, than young people realize. It's harder to take a glass down from the shelf for fear of breaking it. It's harder to pour a hot cup of coffee, and it's harder to clean up the crumbs after making a sandwich. And every day, it gets harder to remember what pants and shirt he wore yesterday. "I shouldn't have to admit that I can't do at 84 what I did before. You ought to know it . . . Maybe when they get to be my age, they'll say, 'I know what he means.' But I'll be molding in the grave." Maybe 25 years from now, he says, Georgia or Leila will think back on their dead dad. "And they can be more tolerant of their children."

He tells a story: When he was a minister in Augusta, he had elderly congregants who couldn't get out of bed to eat or go to the bathroom. "If you have one on your hands," he says, "don't make them concede they have the problem. They know. Don't frown every time they call. Turnabout is fair play. Time is passing for me, but it's also passing for you . . . I'd hate to have Leila or Georgia put me in the bathtub when I was naked. I'd hate that. I still have my pride . . . I don't worry about it, but I think about it. And I believe if I come to that place, they'd do it . . . I believe this is life. You have to take it as you find it."

The reverend sits forward in his chair, straightens his back, says, "There's one thing you have to know." As he speaks, his voice goes deep and clear and his arms gesture in grand designs.

"My latest sun is sinking fast,
My race is nearly run.

My strongest trials now are past,
My triumph is begun.
I know I'm nearing the holy ranks
Of friend and kindred dear.
I brush the dew on Jordan's banks;
The crossing must be near."

The reverend stops, pauses for a long moment. "I may be here tomorrow. I may not." He leans forward, cocks his head and smiles.

"I'm sorry if I bored you."

# A PERSON WHO WANTED TO BE FREE

Rosa Parks was not a simple woman. She wasn't meek. She was no more tired that day than usual. She had forethought aplenty when she refused to surrender her bus seat to a white man. We know it now as an American moment of awakening and reckoning. But the history of that moment is more complex.

Bus No. 5726: A shell, really, a decaying hulk with its glass eyes missing from their windshield sockets, red rust marching like a conquering fungus from its roof, down and around bullet-pocked windows to its faded green and yellow sides. An era's relic, stored in the wind, rain and stultifying summer sun on the vo-tech school's back lot, stored on the chance that the people of Montgomery, Alabama, will someday reach a place in mind and heart where they will find, who knows, $100,000 to refurbish it as a lesson from that night 40 years ago, December 1, 1955, when a city bus driver asked a prim Black woman to leave her window seat so that a white man could sit, and she uttered an almost inaudible, "No." It was an ordinary evening, Christmas lights flickering, people hurrying home past the banner "Peace on Earth, Goodwill to Men." Even Rosa Parks, 42 then, was thinking about all she had to do in the next few days. But at the instant she refused to move, as Eldridge Cleaver once said, "Somewhere in the universe, a gear in the machinery shifted." The wonder of it: Imagine the chances that so precise a moment of reckoning would be encoded in our collective consciousness. Stop time: Look back, look ahead, jot a note, nothing will ever be the same. The stopwatch of history has been pressed now, at this instant of resonance, this flash of leavening light.

Bus No. 5726: It is not the bus—the bus is long lost. After all, that December 1 trip seemed like just another run on the Cleveland Avenue line. Business as usual. But this artifact from that time, most of its seats now gone, is still a narrow passageway from then to now, a time-tunnel. Scores of wasps inhabit the place, a few flying in and out of the missing windows, most huddling and pulsing en masse on their nests. A headlight that will never again illuminate languishes on a mantel behind the long rear seat, which was always occupied by "coloreds." The dust on that seat and others, the dust on the floor, is so thick that the interior is like a sidewalk caked with dry, powdery dirt after a flood. On the filthy floor is a red plastic bucket marked by the moment the white paint was last poured from it. Small hinges and a batch of tiny screws are strewn haphazardly about, as if a conjurer had, with the flick of a wrist, tossed them there like metal bones in an effort to read some meaning into it all, discern the mystery.

The smells are of age and dust and raging summer heat, the lessons are of change and intransigence so great it is hard now even to comprehend. The dirty air tightens the lungs, like breathing gravel. A seat is torn in a cut-away display: old wood, followed by coarse dark fiber, followed by soft white stuffing—the hidden layers, like those of America, finally laid bare.

"A gear in the machinery shifted."

Yes, but why?

Why Montgomery? Why 1955?

Most of all, why Rosa Parks?

"Yeah, I know'd her," says A.T. Boswell, an erect 79-year-old man poised in front of his house, a hardscrabble house with a tin roof and a tilting chimney that sits beneath a huge sheltering water oak in Pine Level, Ala., precisely 20 miles southeast of Montgomery on Route 231. It was a long distance for Rosa Parks and America to travel. In bib overalls, Mr. Boswell stands with his giant hands planted powerfully on his hips, his eyes clear, his long face narrow at the chin and wide at the forehead, a triangle standing on its tip. A thin scar, evidence of a bout with a barbed wire fence decades ago, runs the length of his left forearm. His voice, from deep in his chest, seems to roil his words before they arrive, creating a dialect almost too foreign for a stranger.

"She's related to my people," he says of Rosa Parks.

"Who was her mama?" asks Julia Boswell, Mr. Boswell's wife of 52 years. She has joined him in the sunny yard, her hands clasped casually behind her back. At 69, she is short, round and relaxed to Mr. Boswell's tall, gaunt and formal. She wears a denim hat with a round brim that casts a shadow over her face, a blue-and-white house dress and a white apron. Beyond the house, her laundry is drying on the line. Mr. Boswell rumbles a response.

"Oh, Leona!" Mrs. Boswell interprets. "Leona and cousin Fannie were sisters. Well, his grandmother was they aunt. She was Leona Edwards' aunt. That was Rosa Parks's mother."

"She was raised on the farm," says Mr. Boswell.

Rosa Parks was born in Tuskegee, Ala., in 1913. By the time she was a toddler, the marriage of her mother and father was pretty much over and Leona had moved back to Pine Level to live with her parents. Leona wasn't your average country woman. She was a schoolteacher who had attended the private Payne University in Selma at a time when public education for most of Alabama's Black children ended in the sixth grade. Unlike nearly all Black families near Pine Level, Leona's family didn't crop for shares. The family owned 12 acres of land that one of Rosa's great-grandfathers, a Scotch-Irish indentured servant, had bought after the Civil War and another six acres one of her grandmothers had inherited from the family of a white girl she'd once cared for. In that time and place, the family of Rosa Parks was comfortable.

While many Blacks then felt compelled to smile and shuffle around whites, such behavior was banned in her home. Rosa's maternal grandfather, the son of a white plantation owner and a seamstress house slave, had been mistreated terribly as a boy by a plantation overseer and he hated whites. He wouldn't let Rosa and her brother, Sylvester, play with them. Rosa once stayed up late with him as he sat resolutely, shotgun at the ready, while the Ku Klux Klan rode the countryside. He told her he'd shoot the first Klansman through the door. Her grandfather was so light-skinned that he could easily pass for white, and he took joy in reaching out and shaking the hands of white strangers, calling them by their first names and introducing himself by his last name, dangerous violations of racist protocol at the time.

Young Rosa took her cues from her grandfather and stood up to white children who tried to bully her, although her grandmother warned that she'd get herself lynched someday. That Rosa had white ancestors on her mother's side and her father's side made the hard line between Black and white seem even more ludicrous. As a girl, she secretly admired a dark-skinned Pine Level man who always refused to work for whites. Years later, one of the traits that attracted her to her future husband, Raymond, was that he had faced down white bullies and even helped raise money for the defense of the Scottsboro Boys, nine Black Alabama youths convicted in 1931 on flimsy evidence for supposedly raping two white women.

Rosa was a quiet, polite girl, petite and delicate. She played tag, hide-and-seek and Rise Sally Rise with the other kids but wasn't much of a rough-houser, played a lousy game of baseball. She had a sweet voice, loved to sing gospel in church, read the Bible to her grandmother after her eyes failed. Rosa's mother expected her children to excel in school. Rotha Boswell, a cousin of Rosa's who is now 81, even remembers a time Leona spanked Rosa's brother for getting lower marks than Rotha, who always thought Leona believed her children were better than everybody else's.

The strength and confidence of Rosa Parks and her family don't exactly jibe with the Rosa Parks myth—the myth that emerged from her refusal to move to the back of the bus in 1955, the myth that served the needs of the emergent civil rights movement and the myth that spoke so eloquently to Black and white America: She was a poor, simple seamstress, Rosa Parks, humble and gentle, no rabble-rouser, a meek Negro woman, exhausted from a hard day's work, a woman who had been abused and humiliated by segregation one time too many, who without forethought chose to sit her ground.

In truth, Rosa Parks was far more and far less than the mythology that engulfed her and that became the mobilizing metaphor of the Montgomery bus boycott, which lasted 381 days, raised the unknown Rev. Martin Luther King Jr. to international prominence and helped launch the modern civil rights movement.

Rosa Parks was not a simple woman. She wasn't meek. She was no more tired that day than usual. She had forethought aplenty. She didn't start the Montgomery bus boycott or the civil rights movement, neither of which burst forth from any single symbolic act. Forty years later, the defiance of Rosa Parks and the success of the boycott are enshrined in mystery and myth that obscure a deeper truth that is even richer, grander and more heroic. "I know you won't write this," says Aldon Morris, sociologist and author of *Origins of the Civil Rights Movement*, "but what Rosa Parks did is really the least significant part of the story. She refused to give up her seat and was arrested. I'm not even completely comfortable with deflating the myth. What I'm trying to say is we take that action, elevate it to epic proportions, but all the things that happened so she could become epic, we drop by the wayside . . . That she was just a sweet lady who was tired is the myth . . . The real story of Montgomery is that real people with frailties made change.

"That's what the magic is."

Back in her front yard, Mrs. Boswell waves her hand in the air to stop the conversation, walks toward the porch to fetch her purse and says, "I'm gonna take you to someone else's house." No place is more than a few minutes away in Pine Level, but the trip detours to the Mount Zion African Methodist Episcopal Church on old Route 231, where the Boswells, Rosa Parks and just about every Black resident of Pine Level have always gone to church. The original frame church, where Rosa Parks's uncle was the pastor, is gone, replaced with a utilitarian cinder block church, stark white.

The church is locked and she and her husband walk through the shady graveyard north of the church. They look for stone markers with the names of Mrs. Parks's forebears, but find none. "We didn't have markers then," says Mrs. Boswell, her purse slung over her left shoulder and tucked neatly under her arm. "A lot ain't got no markers now. They just buried in the dirt. Then forgot 'em and buried somebody else on top of 'em. That's the way it be . . . I got a grandmother and grandfather out here and I don't know where they at. Since my mother passed, I don't know where they at." If Mrs. Boswell's mother, who died in 1958, were alive today, she'd think the change in race relations since 1955 was a miracle. "She wouldn't a believed it," Mrs. Boswell says with finality. After a pause, she says, "I wouldn't a believed it either." She, too, believes it was a miracle.

"White men here," Mrs. Boswell says, as she walks from grave to grave, "they kilt an innocent bystander boy, buried right down there." She points to a corner of the graveyard. She figures it was in the '30s. "His last name was Palmer, Otis Palmer, or something. He's probably in one a them that ain't got no stone." A white gang was searching for a Black they believed had killed a white man. "And this boy was out there some kinda way and got kilt. I imagine they mighta thought he was the Black man did it, you know? They just shot 'im . . . I know the day. I was a kid then myself."

At the nearby home of their friends, Mr. Boswell walks past the little trailer where they live, past Black Boy, the frail old dog sleeping at the steps, and out to the place where Eugene Percival is sitting in a rusty metal chair on pale dirt that is packed as hard as concrete. He, too, wears bib overalls. He is 85 years old: "I tell ya when I was born, ought 9." For a moment, the old men talk to each other in a dialect almost too foreign for a stranger.

"Rosa Parks, my dad's her uncle," Mr. Percival finally says, bobbing his head, his right leg crossed at the knee over his left, his posture that of a much younger man. "Oh, she was mean, mean as could be." He leans forward, laughs at his own teasing, and says seriously, "She was a good woman. And still good, ain't she?"

From the trailer, Mr. Percival's sister-in-law, Ina Mae Gray, 92 years old, is making her way slowly and painfully across the pale dirt. She's a large woman with a bandanna wrapped around her head and another bandanna tied western-style around her neck. She, too, sits in a metal chair. "Arthritis," she says, pulling up her long dress to her knees, running her hands gently down over her calves and then stopping to massage the bridges of her feet. She glances up askance at the white stranger and flashes a wary smile: "You're not gonna put me in jail, are ya? I don't wanta see the jail, noooo!" Mrs. Gray, too, remembers Rosa Parks. "She was a good child, go to the field and hoe and plow. Pickin' cotton . . . And anything else you could raise to eat . . . I know'd her mama. What's her mama's name?"

"Leona," says Mr. Boswell.

"I heared that 'bout the bus," says Mrs. Gray. "She was tryin' to get us a livin', I reckon." And suddenly, Mrs. Gray is angry, her voice rising. "Let us have som'in' like them . . . Woooo, man, man! I had a hard time, hell, try to eat and couldn't eat. Had to eat water and bread and all kinda mess." Her face is contorted now and she is fighting back tears, her voice trembling. "They was over us, they might beat our ass and go to cussin'." How is she supposed to love white people? Mrs. Gray asks. "Man, I could cry! Right now! The way they done us. Let's call it: Us didn't have nothin'."

"Hard times!" Mr. Percival says.

Mrs. Gray gets wary again: "Don't put me in jail, mister."

From the trailer, Mrs. Boswell and Mr. Percival's wife, Nettie Mae, who is 81, come out to join the conversation. Mrs. Percival says she wasn't surprised when Rosa Parks got arrested. On any given day, because of the way it was, any Black person could've snapped, met their limit and gone off, boom!

"They treated ya like slaves!" says Mrs. Boswell.

"I coulda did it," Mrs. Percival says, her eyes wide and intense.

Everyone nods in agreement.

Mrs. Boswell: "It's over with now."

Mr. Boswell: "Time and God changed that."

Cloverdale is a beautiful Montgomery neighborhood of land-scaped yards, mature trees, flowering bushes, old, elegant homes. Cloverdale, which is integrated today, speaks to the incongruence that is the life of Virginia Durr, a 92-year-old white woman and daughter of Montgomery's gentry who, with her husband, Clifford, was one of the few whites brave or committed or foolish enough to support Rosa Parks and the bus boycott. Her husband's law practice was nearly ruined, two of her daughters had to be sent to school up North, her yard was littered with obscene leaflets.

Mrs. Durr, a widow for 20 years, has been helped into the car from her small, white-clapboard retirement home. Her wheelchair is packed in the trunk. She is waiting for her friend and paid helper, Zecozy Williams, a 77-year-old Black woman, to close up the house and climb in the car. Rather than talk in the house, Mrs. Durr prefers to go out for dinner. She has a huddled, little-old-lady look about her as she sits, her snowy hair swept up nicely, her hands smoothing the lap of her flowered skirt. But as she explains her choice of restaurant, her sing-song Southern voice carrying a pleasant archness, she doesn't sound like a little old lady.

"It's just that at certain restaurants you're more welcome than at others," she says, referring to Mrs. Williams. "Certain places are white places and certain places are Black places. And so when you find one that will welcome both, you're lucky." Mrs. Durr has selected the Sahara. "They have Black waiters . . . If they have Black waiters, she's more comfortable than if they have white waiters."

Has Mrs. Williams actually told her this?

Mrs. Durr smiles benevolently. "No, honey, I know it."

On the night Rosa Parks was arrested, Eddie Mae Pratt, now 79 and a friend of a friend of Mrs. Parks, happened to be on the crowded bus. She was standing in the rear and couldn't see the commotion up front. Word filtered back that a Black woman wouldn't give up her seat to a white. Mrs. Pratt, who knew Mrs. Parks from evenings she spent sewing clothing with Bertha T. Butler, Mrs. Pratt's neighbor, finally caught a glimpse of Mrs. Parks as she was led off the bus. Suddenly, she felt weak. She wrapped her arms around her chest and when the bus lurched forward, she slipped hard enough that a Black man offered her his seat and she sat down.

"Do you feel all right?" he asked.

"That's Mrs. Parks," she said, stunned.

At her stop, Mrs. Pratt ran to the nearby house of Bertha Butler, who said, "Oh, my goodness!" She called the home of E.D. Nixon, the founder and former president of the Montgomery NAACP, where Mrs. Parks had been the volunteer secretary for 12 years. Nixon called Clifford Durr, who knew Mrs. Parks because, upon Nixon's recommendation, she had been doing seamstress work for Mrs. Durr. When Nixon drove by to pick up Clifford Durr, Mrs. Durr was with him and they went and bailed out Mrs. Parks.

Forty years later, at the Sahara, where Mrs. Durr is seated in her wheelchair at the table and Mrs. Williams is helping cut her entree, an old Black waiter whispers to a young Black waiter: "That's Mrs. Durr, who went and got Rosa Parks out of jail."

Mrs. Durr smiles. "My claim to fame."

That's not exactly true. Clifford Durr, who grew up in Montgomery, was a Rhodes scholar with a law degree from Oxford University and a New Dealer whom Franklin Roosevelt had appointed to the Federal Communications Commission. After Clifford resigned to represent people charged as subversives in the communist witch hunts of the 1950s, the Durrs returned to their home town, where his family was the founder and owner of the prosperous Durr drugstore chain. Although politically conservative, the family supported Clifford and Virginia financially and gave him legal business. Then Virginia and Clifford were tarred as alleged communist sympathizers by U.S. Sen. James Eastland of Mississippi, whom an outraged Clifford publicly challenged to a fistfight. The Durrs were ostracized in elite Montgomery society, especially after it became known that Mrs. Durr was holding interracial women's prayer gatherings in their home. She once called to confirm a birthday party invitation sent to one of their daughters.

"Are you Clifford Durr's wife?" a man asked.

"Yes."

"Well, Mrs. Durr, no child of yours can enter this house."

Through a New Deal acquaintance, Clifford met E.D. Nixon, who is perhaps the most unsung of Montgomery's civil rights heroes. He was a Pullman porter and the local head of A. Philip Randolph's powerful Brotherhood of Sleeping Car Porters. Nixon was close to Randolph, who in the '40s was already calling for massive grass-roots demonstrations against Southern Jim Crow laws. Nixon himself had opened the local NAACP chapter in the 1920s. In Montgomery, Nixon was "Mr. Civil Rights." He was rough-edged and poorly spoken, but he was an indefatigable man bravely willing to call public attention to the constant abuse of Black people.

In those days, there was only one Black lawyer in Montgomery. So when Nixon learned that Clifford Durr would take Black clients, he sent them to him—no doubt also hoping to create a powerful white friend and ally. When Clifford mentioned that his wife needed a seamstress to alter the clothing their daughters received as hand-me-downs from rich relations—including Virginia's sister, the wife of former U.S. senator and then-Supreme Court Justice Hugo L. Black—Nixon sent Mrs. Parks, who had become a woman in the mold of the girl she had been.

Rosa Parks was pretty, with supple, tan skin and brown hair that ran to near her waist when it was down, but which in public was always braided and rolled in the fashion of Scarlett O'Hara in *Gone With the Wind*. She wore little makeup. She had a lovely smile and a gentle laugh, although folks can't remember her ever telling a joke or talking about a favorite movie. They can't remember her ever dancing or playing cards. She never gossiped, never seemed to get angry or even exasperated. She had flawless diction and elegant penmanship. Although she spoke little, she was gently assertive when she did, with a touch of music in her voice. Her long silences weren't uncomfortable. She was a serene, placid woman whose quietness was easily mistaken for timidity.

"She was very much a lady," says Mrs. Durr, who has only nibbled at her dinner. "The thing that makes it so interesting is that a lot of white women, they came down here after the Civil War and started a school, and she had gone to that school . . . staffed by white women, high-class women who came down to the South to be missionaries to the Blacks." It was the Montgomery Industrial School for girls—dubbed Miss White's school after its headmistress, Alice L. White. Rosa's mother had sent her to live with Montgomery relatives so she could attend. Rosa cleaned classrooms to help pay her way. It's believed that Miss White's school got money from Sears, Roebuck & Co. chairman Julius Rosenwald, who funded schools for Blacks all across the South. "She came from good people and she had all the elements of a lady," Mrs. Durr says of Mrs. Parks. "Neatness and order—just a lovely person."

After dinner, Zecozy Williams packs Mrs. Durr's meal into a doggie box. Back at home, before she sits down to talk about Rosa Parks and the boycott, Mrs. Williams helps Mrs. Durr get comfortably situated in her living room on the couch beneath an oil painting of herself. While Mrs. Durr reads *Wallis and Edward*, the story of the Prince of Wales and Wallis Warfield Simpson, Mrs. Williams goes to the dining room, sits in a large rose-colored wing chair and mends one of Mrs. Durr's bathrobes. She's getting Mrs. Durr ready for her summer trip to Martha's Vineyard. "This is what Rosa did," Mrs. Williams says, laughing, her voice rich and deep and liquid. "I'm doin' the same thing."

Mrs. Williams didn't know Rosa Parks well. She, too, had moved to Montgomery from a country town, Hope Hull, Ala., but she was from a dirt-poor cropping family. As a teenager, she kept house for a white doctor in the country—cooked three meals a day, cleaned the house and did the laundry for $5 a week. She also carried eggs, 15 to 20 dozen, into Montgomery on horseback to sell. Then she started taking a bus into the city to do domestic work for $3 a day. It was hard for her to catch the bus on time, because her family didn't own a clock. In 1950, she and her husband moved to Montgomery.

One day, the woman doing her hair, Bertha Smith, asked if Mrs. Williams was a registered voter. "I didn't know what that was. Really, I didn't." But soon she was attending voting clinics run by Rufus Lewis, a former teacher and football coach at what is today Alabama State University, Montgomery's historically Black college. As the NAACP was E.D. Nixon's mission, voter registration was the mission of Rufus Lewis. The men were rival leaders, Lewis said to represent Blacks teaching or educated at Alabama State and Nixon said to represent working people like himself. The saying was: Nixon had the "masses" and Lewis had the "classes." Through Nixon, Zecozy Williams met Rosa Parks, who in 1943 had become the NAACP secretary in the footsteps of Johnnie Carr, a friend and fellow classmate from Miss White's school whose son would later become the test case that desegregated Montgomery's public schools. Before long,

Mrs. Williams was helping Nixon and Lewis teach Black folks how to pass the dreaded Alabama literacy test.

"I never did get afraid," Mrs. Williams says, even when she returned to Hope Hull and began registering Blacks. Why? She doesn't know. She just put fear out of her mind, flicked a switch. After a while, she went to a white county politician and told him a new road was needed running out to the Black schoolhouse.

"How many people you got registered?" he asked.

"Well, we got quite a few."

"Name some of 'em."

She did.

Mrs. Williams stops sewing. "And he made a road, ditched it on both sides." She is still incredulous. "And that was because of me. That was the first time I saw the power."

In the early '50s, Mrs. Williams occasionally served at Mrs. Durr's parties. She was already the full-time domestic for Mr. Durr's sister and her husband, Stanhope Elmore. She liked the Elmores, but it was Mrs. Durr she admired. "Mr. Elmore and them would talk about her," she says. "She was an outcast. They never invited them over." But Black people, whether or not they knew her personally, understood that Virginia Durr was putting her life and the lives of her family on the line. Mrs. Williams nods toward the old woman reading in the living room: "Mrs. Durr is a brave woman."

The east side of old Black Montgomery isn't what it used to be. Alabama State still anchors the neighborhood, but many affluent Blacks have migrated to the suburbs, where they now live among whites. Many doctors and lawyers, even public school teachers with two modest incomes have abandoned Montgomery's old Black neighborhoods. But Rufus Lewis, 88 years old, a giant in the Montgomery civil rights movement, a man barely known outside his circle of aged contemporaries, still lives on the old Black east side. He looks remarkably like the young, imperious Rufus Lewis, his head still kingly and dignified, with the bearing of an old, unbowed lion. But his mind is cloudy. He can't recall his past. He can't recall Rosa Parks.

Back in the '40s, Lewis became obsessed with Black voting rights. Night after night, he traveled the countryside teaching Blacks how to register. In Montgomery, he founded the Citizens Club, a private nightclub Blacks could join only if they were registered voters. An entire generation of Montgomery Blacks say Rufus Lewis is the reason they first voted. Lewis was the first to ramrod the Montgomery bus boycott's labyrinthine automobile transport system that helped get Black boycotters back and forth every day for 13 months. Lewis, with Nixon's concurrence, nominated Martin Luther King Jr. to head the organization leading the boycott.

"Tell him as much as you remember, Daddy," says his 56-year-old daughter, Eleanor Dawkins. She sits in her father's knotty pine study with his old friend, a former mailman and present Montgomery City Council president, 73-year-old Joseph Dickerson. "I thought that with Joe here," his daughter says, "maybe there will be something that will come up."

"Maybe," Mr. Lewis says tentatively.

"He believed," says Mr. Dickerson, who took part in five major European operations in World War II, "that if you go off to fight for your country, you oughta be able to vote in your country."

Something stirs in Mr. Lewis. "We got a lotta folks registered," he says, smiling. They mimeographed the literacy test, taught folks the answers, traveled by cover of night through the backwoods Jim Crow landscape, sent light-skinned Blacks to the Montgomery registrar's office to learn if it was open that day, drove folks to the courthouse. When people failed the test—as they usually did the first time or two—Lewis and his workers did it all again, and then again. He stops talking, leans across the desk where he is sitting, fingers steepled, eyes blank, lost again.

Does Mr. Lewis know that history records his achievements?

"Well, that's fine to be remembered in the books," he says, suddenly firm and lucid, "but the best part of it was being there to help the people who needed help . . . That was our job."

The night Rosa Parks was arrested, E.D. Nixon and Clifford Durr recognized instinctively that Mrs. Parks was the vessel they'd been seeking to challenge the segregated bus laws. Other Blacks had been arrested for defying those laws. Only months before, a 15-year-old girl, Claudette Colvin—inspired by a high school teacher's lectures on the need for equal rights, angered by the conviction of a Black high school student for allegedly raping a white woman—had refused to give up her seat to a white, then resisted arrest when the police came. She kept hollering, "It's my constitutional right!" Nixon had decided against contesting her case: She had fought with police, she came from the poorer side of Black Montgomery and, it was later learned, she was pregnant. He had also rejected the cases of several other women recently arrested, waiting for just the right vessel to arrive.

Then came Mrs. Parks. "We got a lady can't nobody touch," Nixon said. There were other advantages. Rosa Parks, because of her well-mannered, serene demeanor, her proper speech, her humble, saintly way, her ascetic lifestyle—she didn't drink, smoke or curse—carried not only the image but the reality of the deserving Negro. Mrs. Parks had the qualities middle-class whites claimed in themselves and denied in Blacks. Nothing about her supported the white contention that she deserved to be treated as inferior.

She had another advantage: Although whites may have viewed Blacks as a single entity, the social class fissures within the Black community—between educated and uneducated, affluent and poor—ran deep. Mrs. Parks bridged that gap: She was of "working-class station and middle-class demeanor," as Taylor Branch wrote in *Parting the Waters*. She came from a good family, her relatives were prominent in Montgomery's St. Paul AME Church, she was educated at Miss White's and later Alabama State's lab school, and she had the manners—as Virginia Durr said—of a "lady." In her role as NAACP secretary, she was respected by the city's educated activist community. But she was also a seamstress who earned $23 a week, whose fingers and feet were tired from honest work. She was a PR bonanza—with a bonus.

She was velvet hiding steel.

That night, after hushed conversations, Nixon and Clifford Durr asked if she would plead not guilty and fight her arrest in court. Nixon said they could take the case to the Supreme Court. Her husband,

Raymond, a barber, was terrified, and Mrs. Durr later recalled in her memoir, *Outside the Magic Circle*, that he kept saying, "Rosa, the white folks will kill you! Rosa, the white folks will kill you!" Like a chant. Mrs. Parks was perfectly calm.

"I'll go along with you, Mr. Nixon."

Her decision wasn't as simple as it seems, wasn't made in that one instant, but was a long time coming. In her 1992 autobiography, *Rosa Parks: My Story*, the source for many of the details about her life and attitudes, Mrs. Parks writes that as she sat on the bus, waiting for the police to arrive, she was thinking about the night as a girl when she sat with her grandfather, shotgun at the ready, while the KKK rode the countryside. The humiliating segregation of Montgomery's buses was much on her mind. Not only had Claudette Colvin's arrest occurred last spring, but just a month earlier, a bus driver had ordered Mrs. Parks's dear friend, Bertha Butler, to move back to make room for a white man: "You sit back there with the niggers." Mrs. Butler was a woman raising two children on her own, who also worked as a seamstress, who sometimes sewed until 5 a.m. for extra income and who still found time to run voter clinics in her home two nights a week. She had befriended Mrs. Parks because she so admired her civil rights work. Mrs. Butler didn't move at the order, and the standing white man, in soldier's uniform, had intervened: "That's your seat and you sit there." Mrs. Butler, now retired at age 76 and living near Philadelphia, was glad she wasn't the one to get arrested. "God looked at me and said I wasn't strong enough," she says. "Mrs. Parks was the person."

At the time Mrs. Parks was arrested, she was in the process of rejuvenating the NAACP's youth organization, getting ready for a conference in a few days. Only the summer before, at the behest of Virginia Durr, Mrs. Parks had spent 10 days at the interracial Highlander Folk School in Tennessee, a labor organizing camp that had turned its radical eye on civil rights. Mrs. Parks loved waking up in the morning at Highlander, smelling the bacon and eggs cooking—and knowing it was white people fixing breakfast for her. She returned home, Mrs. Durr later said, inspired at realizing that whites and Blacks could live as equals and even more disgusted with segregation. One of Highlander's most famous Black teachers, Septima Clark, said later, "Rosa Parks was afraid for white people to know that she was as militant as she was."

Mrs. Parks had been training her high school charges in the ways of civil disobedience. Mrs. Butler's 58-year-old daughter, Zynobia Tatum, remembers saying to Mrs. Parks, "They are going to hit me, spit on me and call me names, and I can't fight back? I cannot promise you." Mrs. Parks told Zynobia she needed more training. Already, Mrs. Parks had sent her youth group members into the whites-only public library to order books. Zynobia Tatum recalls that she and Mrs. Parks had often taken drinks from whites-only water fountains downtown—"to show our disapproval." After Claudette Colvin's arrest for refusing to give up her seat, Claudette joined Mrs. Parks's group—and Mrs. Parks discovered she was the great-granddaughter of the dark-skinned Black man in Pine Level who had refused to work for whites, the man young Rosa had secretly admired. It was almost prophetic.

Despite her genuine gentleness and pragmatic faith in the tactic of civil disobedience, Rosa Parks was never entirely comfortable with the philosophy of nonviolence and the idea that if Black people were attacked, they shouldn't fight back. In an obscure 1967 interview on file at Howard University she said bluntly, "I don't believe in gradualism or that whatever is to be done for the better should take forever to do."

For more than a decade as NAACP secretary, she had watched case after case of injustice against Blacks come through the NAACP office, almost all of which she was powerless to change. She'd worked with a group trying to save the life of the young Montgomery man convicted of raping a white woman—the case that had so outraged Claudette Colvin—only to see him executed. She knew the widow and three small children of a Black man who, in his U.S. military uniform, was shot dead by police after he supposedly caused a scene on a Montgomery bus. She had told local NAACP board member Frank Bray, now 75, that someone needed to do something to break the fist of segregation, even if it meant a sacrifice.

"I had no idea," he says, "that she would be the sacrificial lamb . . . She'd say, 'These folks have all these beautiful churches and they profess to be Christians and yet they have businesses where the clerks are not courteous and where you cannot use a restroom and if you drink water you have to drink out of the little spigot that was added to the main fountain' . . . Most Blacks resented the conditions and many of them adjusted to it and many did not adjust. She did not adjust." After her arrest, Mrs. Parks revealed to fellow boycott worker Hazel Gregory, now 75, that she had thought about refusing to give up her seat in the past.

Montgomery whites claimed that her arrest was part of a plot, that Nixon had put his longtime secretary up to it. No evidence supports that claim. On the night of her arrest, Nixon was shocked and confused, flailing about in his effort to get her released. It is embedded in the American psyche that Rosa Parks acted on the spur of the moment, and her arrest is often called the "spark" that ignited the modern civil rights movement. In fact, Rosa Parks's act and the firestorm that followed were more like spontaneous combustion— a fire ignited by the buildup of heat over time in material ripe for explosion. Mrs. Parks, who wasn't afraid as she waited for her arrest, who felt oddly serene, revealed the lifetime thread of experiences that had led to her action when the police arrived and asked once more if she would move. In the way of the Bible, she answered with a question:

"Why do you all push us around?"

No moral philosopher, the cop said, "I don't know."

Then she was led away.

Years later, Edward Warren Boswell, now 41, the son of a cousin Mrs. Parks grew up with in Pine Level, asked her why she refused to move that particular day. "She said she had no idea," he recalls. His 44-year-old sister, Betty Boswell, says, "She said she was just tired from working, and they had always been harassing Black people about not sitting to the front and she said that particular day she just wasn't in the mood . . . Her feet were hurting." Mrs. Parks told Edward: "It was just set in motion by God."

Back in the study of Rufus Lewis, City Council President Joe Dickerson agrees. But he, like Mrs. Parks and almost everybody else who was involved in the boycott, was of the praise-the-Lord-and-pass-the-ammunition school of religion. Every inch of progress was a battle. White politicians tried to break the boycott in court, and the boycott leaders fought back in court. The white thugs bombed four churches and the homes of King, Nixon and Ralph Abernathy, a young minister in Montgomery at the time. As Zecozy Williams said, people risked their lives.

Theirs was an eerie determination. King later wrote that he was increasingly afraid until late one night when he felt the presence and the resoluteness of God descend upon him. Mrs. Williams said she flicked a mental switch to turn off her fear. Mrs. Parks described her serenity as she waited to be arrested. And now, Mr. Dickerson compares his state of mind during the dangerous days of the boycott to the way he felt the night before a military operation in World War II: "Gotta go."

Mr. Dickerson: "It's a miracle."

Mr. Lewis: "I just feel grateful that we came through."

The room is like Inez Baskin's private museum. The large portrait of her grandfather stands on an easel. In his bow tie and vest, with his mustache and slicked-back hair, he looks every bit an Irishman. The photo of her mother and father, so fair-skinned, sits on the piano encased in plastic wrap for protection. "My husband's father was white, too," she says. And of course, on the wall, is the famous photo of Mrs. Baskin, now 79 years old, on the day that bus segregation ended in Montgomery: Mrs. Baskin, Abernathy, King and two others riding a bus. The photo ran worldwide, and Inez Baskin, a reporter for the "colored page" of the *Montgomery Advertiser* and a correspondent for *Jet* magazine and the *Pittsburgh Courier*, was mistaken by many for Rosa Parks, still is today.

"In the '50s, I didn't have any sense," she says, sitting in a large, comfortable chair amid her memorabilia. She softly rubs her face, plays with the ring on her left hand. Her long gray hair sweeps over from the right, dangling in a single braid to her left. She speaks softly and deliberately. "I thought I could walk on water in those days." With a Black photographer, she once raced out to Prattville, Ala., after a report that the Klan was burning a cross. The crowd was gone, but the cross was still burning. She laughs and shakes her head at the memory. A photo ran in *Jet*.

Did she know Rosa Parks?

She smiles faintly. "An angel walking."

"I wonder sometimes what it would have taken just to make her act like the rest of us . . . She would smile, very demure, and never raise her voice. She was just different in a very angelic way . . . 'If you can walk with kings and not lose the common touch.' Those are the kind of expressions that come to mind when you think about Rosa Parks. My great-grandmother had an expression for it: 'living on earth and boarding in Glory.' "

Mrs. Baskin believes Mrs. Parks was heaven-sent?

"She had to be."

On the night Rosa Parks was arrested, after she had agreed to become bus segregation's test case, 24-year-old Fred Gray, one of Montgomery's two Black attorneys then, arrived home late from out of town and got the word. Gray had grown up in Montgomery, attended Alabama State and gone to Ohio for law school because Alabama didn't have a law school for Blacks. When the state required five attorneys to sign character affidavits before he could practice, Gray had gone to E.D. Nixon, who helped him find the lawyers. One of them was Clifford Durr. Gray had returned home with one goal— to "destroy everything segregated." Mrs. Parks immediately offered her services. Every day, she came to his downtown office at lunch, answered his mail for free, encouraged his idealism. They talked not only about the buses, but inferior Black schools, segregated parks, swimming pools and toilets. In his memoir, *Bus Ride to Justice*, Gray, now 64, later wrote, "She gave me the feeling that I was the Moses that God had sent to Pharaoh."

Fred Gray upped the ante. Late on the night Mrs. Parks was arrested, he visited Jo Ann Robinson, an Alabama State professor and president of the Women's Political Council, a group composed of female university professors, public school teachers, nurses, social workers and the wives of Montgomery's Black professional men. For months, Robinson had been laying plans for a bus boycott. Although she and most of Montgomery's affluent Blacks owned cars and didn't ride the buses often, she had taken a bus to the airport in 1949 and mistakenly sat in a white seat. The driver went wild, screamed, threatened. "I felt like a dog," she later said.

Every Black person who rode a bus had a tale to tell: the man who paid his last coin in fare only to have the bus drive off before he could return and enter through the back door, the woman who was attacked when she stepped onto a bus to pay ahead of a white man, the pregnant woman who fell when a bus pulled away as she stepped off. In 1953 alone, the Women's Council had received 30 complaints from Black bus riders.

It was a unifying indignity.

Inspired by the Supreme Court ruling that had banned "separate but equal" schools in 1954, Robinson had even written the mayor and warned that if Black riders weren't treated more courteously "twenty-five or more local organizations" were planning a bus boycott. It was a hopeful time. Already, a boycott in Baton Rouge, La., organized by the Rev. T.J. Jemison, had won concessions for Black riders in that city. And in Little Rock, Ark., officials had devised a plan to integrate its schools. But nothing had come of Robinson's demands. Then Fred Gray dropped by.

At midnight, Robinson went to Alabama State and furtively used its government-owned paper and mimeograph machines to run off 52,500 leaflets announcing a boycott of Montgomery's buses on the day of Mrs. Parks's trial. The next morning, Robinson and her Women's Council cohorts and students distributed the leaflets to Black schools, stores, taverns, beauty parlors and barber shops. When Alabama State's Black president, H. Councill Trenholm, who served at the pleasure of the Alabama governor, learned of her action, he called her into his office and demanded an explanation. She told him another Black woman had been humiliated on a bus; she promised to pay for the mimeograph paper. He calmed down, warned her to work behind the scenes. Trenholm's wife, too, was a Women's Council member.

The rest is history. Rosa Parks was found guilty and fined $10, plus $4 in court costs. To keep the followers of Rufus Lewis and E.D. Nixon from squabbling, King became the compromise choice to lead the boycott. When Black preachers cozy with Montgomery's powerful whites balked at the idea, Nixon, in his rugged way, questioned their manhood: "You ministers have lived off these wash-women for the last hundred years and ain't never done nothing for them." After Nixon's taunt, King himself said, "Brother Nixon, I'm not a coward." Nixon planted the story of the boycott with a friendly white reporter at the *Montgomery Advertiser*. It became front-page news and announced the boycott to every Black in Montgomery.

There were bombings, threats, lawsuits, harassing phone calls. Victory was not preordained; it came a day at a time. The city's stubborn refusal to compromise on bus seating—other segregated Southern cities didn't have specific seats reserved only for whites—probably hardened the resolve of the boycotters. The bombings certainly turned national public opinion against the segregationists. In 1956, young Fred Gray successfully took his argument against Montgomery's bus segregation to the U.S. Supreme Court. Although many people believe it was Rosa Parks's case that went before the high court, Gray actually didn't use her as a plaintiff because of technicalities in her case that might have undermined his federal lawsuit. Instead, five women whose names are mostly lost to history filed suit: Aurelia Browder, Claudette Colvin, Susie McDonald, Jeanetta Reese and Mary Louise Smith.

Victory had a price: Jo Ann Robinson and about a dozen other activist ASU employees lost their jobs. Monroe J. Gardner, whose granddaughter is now a federal magistrate in Montgomery, used his car to transport people during the boycott. He was beaten. Samuel Patton Sr., a boycott supporter and prominent builder, lost his line of bank credit. E.L. and Dorothy Posey, who ran the only Black-owned parking lot in downtown Montgomery, let their lot be used as a transit staging point. After the boycott, they lost their business. Anne Smith Pratt volunteered dispatching cars to pick up waiting riders. Her marriage ended when her husband was sent overseas and she refused to leave her post. Not to mention the hardships endured by thousands of working-class Blacks who walked miles to work every day in the heat, the cold, the rain. Says sociologist Aldon Morris, "People made this happen."

During the boycott, Rosa Parks helped run the auto dispatch system. She wasn't a leader of the movement, and didn't try to be. She traveled the country raising money. Already, she was a symbol. When she, King and nearly 100 others were charged with conspiracy during the boycott, a photo of her being fingerprinted ran on the front page of the *New York Times*—perhaps because King was out of town and not available to be photographed during his arrest. That picture, mistakenly believed by many to have been taken the night she was first arrested, became a piece of movement iconography.

As the historic significance of the boycott became clearer, as journalists poured in from all over the world, bickering began over the credit. Nixon became jealous of not only King but Rosa Parks. "If it hadn't been for me . . ." he told Mrs. Parks's friend Hazel Gregory. In one of the final recorded interviews of his life in 1988, Nixon told local amateur historian Riley Lewis Jr., "We had court cases that had been filed 10 years 'fore Mrs. Parks was arrested . . . King didn't make the Montgomery bus boycott—me, the peoples and our protest made him!"

He was right. He was wrong.

Everybody made everybody.

Inez Baskin still marvels about those days. "It was as if I was out of myself doing these things," she says, sitting forward in her chair, holding her arms before her and gently swaying, eyes closed. "Not myself, but more myself than ever. It didn't seem as if it was me doing it . . . It was as if we were out of ourselves, watching ourselves . . . Not in our bodies.

"Does that make any sense?"

It is the hands of Rosa Parks that you notice. They are always folded somehow, plaited together so naturally, the left hand lying open on her lap, the right hand's palm lying open over it, her thumb softly massaging her wrist. Or the fingers gently intertwined, her thumbs methodically crossing and recrossing. Or the left palm held open and facing up, the right palm grazing lightly back and forth over its surface. Hands always at rest, always at work.

Rosa Parks is visiting Montgomery today, traveling with a bus tour of youngsters retracing the path of the underground railroad from the South to Canada, stopping at important civil rights sites along the way. The Rosa and Raymond Parks Institute for Self-Development sponsors the tour, which is filled mostly with youths from the Washington and Detroit areas. Mrs. Parks has returned to Montgomery only occasionally since 1957 when she, her husband and her mother moved to Detroit, where her brother lived. She and her husband had lost their jobs and the phone jangled constantly with vicious threats: "You should be killed." Her brother was afraid for them and insisted they move to Detroit, where Mrs. Parks eventually worked for Democratic Rep. John Conyers Jr. as a receptionist and caseworker. She retired in 1988. Her husband, mother and brother are all dead. She is 82.

In cities where she was once despised, she is now treated like royalty—or more. Yesterday in Birmingham, siren-blaring motor-cycle cops stopped traffic for her and the mayor proclaimed it "Rosa Parks Day." At the Birmingham Civil Rights Institute, Mrs. Parks stood quietly looking at a life-sized sculpture of herself sitting on the bus, purse in her lap, staring out the window, waiting to be arrested. Watching her watch herself was an army of TV crews and cameras. In Selma, a woman reached out, took hold of her challis dress and said, "I want to touch the hem of your garment." Unchanged in manner since 1955, Mrs. Parks said, "That's very nice." Today in Montgomery, she is given the key to the city and a speaker intro-duces her by saying, "Why don't we just get on our feet and greet our mother, Rosa Parks!"

The mother of the civil rights movement.

"A saint of American history," a TV reporter calls her.

"I don't consider myself a saint," says Mrs. Parks, who still wears her hair braided and rolled behind her head, still speaks so softly her voice is nearly inaudible, still is velvet hiding steel. "I'm just a person who wanted to be seated on the bus."

But again and again, Rosa Parks tells audiences she didn't remain in her seat because she was physically weary. No, she was weary of the injustice. Again and again, she mentions that she was working at the NAACP before her arrest. No, she didn't plan her arrest, but her whole life from childhood was leading up to it. Without being asked, she is responding to the mythic tale that, ironically, holds her up to worship and diminishes her: the simple seamstress, the meek Negro woman, exhausted from a day's work, who without forethought chose to sit her ground.

Rosa Parks doesn't really answer questions put to her later, questions about why she is often seen as a simple seamstress rather than as an assertive activist, questions about whether her sainthood status diminishes her status as a strong, committed woman. "I was always glad that the people did have the determination to make the sacrifices and take that action," she says in her soft, slow voice. "I just felt that as a person I didn't want to be treated like a second-class citizen. I didn't want to be mistreated under the guise of legally enforced racial segregation and that the more we endured that kind of treatment, the worse we were being treated . . . I consider myself a symbol of freedom and equality, and I wanted to let it be known that that was what I believed in."

It is as simple—and complex—as that.

"She remains a pure symbol," says University of Georgia sociologist Gary Fine, an expert in political symbolism. "For everyone today and in the '50s, it was a text story with only one possible reading— this poor woman who refused to move to the back of the bus. What possible explanation could you possibly have for making her move? It was so transparently egregious." But for a symbol to have 40 years of staying power, Fine says, it must carry a deeper cultural resonance about "our own self-image."

"By protecting this image we are celebrating core values for ourselves as Americans," he says. "There is a universal consensus now that integration is good. She symbolizes this now. Everybody on all sides can use her." For Blacks, she is evidence that they forced change. For whites, she is evidence that they were willing to change.

Rosa Parks as proof: America is good.

"The beauty was that she disappeared from the scene," says Fine, meaning that her later behavior or opinions didn't muddy the purity of her symbolism, as happened with King after allegations of plagiarism and marital infidelity. "She did her duty as a symbol and then disappeared except for ceremonial events."

Back in Montgomery, Mrs. Parks is standing amid the adoration, her hands plaited naturally on the lectern, giving a short talk: She's glad for all the change but more change is needed, the struggle for justice must go on, the greatest power is God. Then, so softly that people must strain to hear, she recites a hymn her mother sang to her as a child in Pine Level:

> O freedom,
> O freedom,
> O freedom over me.
> And before I'd be a slave,
> I'd be buried in my grave,
> And go home to my Lord and be free.

"I'd like for everybody to remember me as a person who wanted to be free."

It is night and Joe Dickerson, the city council president, is standing before bus No. 5726, lit by the headlights of his car. Mr. Dickerson helped get the bus hauled here in hopes that the committee set up to honor the 40th anniversary of the boycott can eventually collect enough private donations to restore it. The Montgomery City Council, with four Blacks and five whites, isn't yet ready to foot the whole bill or to finance the civil rights museum Mr. Dickerson would like to see built inside the old Empire Theater, outside of which Rosa Parks was arrested.

But someday . . .

"If you rode the bus, you were mistreated," Mr. Dickerson says, the light making him look washed and vague and mysterious in his little hat with the brim rolled up all the way around. "And so the time was right. It could have been anybody . . . I guess when the time is right, it's just like Nelson Mandela. If anybody had told Mandela, 'You're gonna be free and you're gonna rule South Africa, man,' you talked like a fool. 'I'm not gonna get outta jail!' So there is a time for everything. And you have to play your role."

Rosa Parks's grandfather who refused to shuffle for whites played his role. So did the dark-skinned man in Pine Level who wouldn't work for whites. Rosa's mother, who sacrificed so Rosa could go to Miss White's school. Miss White. Julius Rosenwald. A. Philip Randolph. The NAACP lawyers who laid decades of groundwork for the 1954 Supreme Court schools decision. The Rev. T.J. Jemison, who organized the earlier Baton Rouge bus boycott. Those who took the literacy test again and again. Raymond Parks. H. Councill Trenholm, Ralph Abernathy, Eddie Mae Pratt, Anne Smith Pratt, E.L. and Dorothy Posey, Zecozy Williams, Bertha Smith, Monroe J. Gardner, Samuel Patton Sr., Johnnie Carr, Bertha T. Butler, Zynobia Tatum, Aurelia Browder, Claudette Colvin, Susie McDonald, Jeanetta Reese, Mary Louise Smith. And, of course, E.D. Nixon, Rufus Lewis, Jo Ann Robinson, Fred Gray, Clifford and Virginia Durr and Martin Luther King Jr., who transformed a demand for seats into a mission for God. And the 40,000 who refused to ride.

Strands in a thread.

Rosa Parks, too, played her role.

She still does.

"The message is ordinary people doing extraordinary things," says sociologist Aldon Morris, who fears that the simplified mythology that enshrouds Rosa Parks and the Montgomery bus boycott, the belief that it was all God-ordained, can obscure the determination, fearlessness and skilled organization of the people who made the movement. "To believe that King or Rosa Parks are heroes, it creates passivity . . . Young people then ask, 'Where's the new Martin Luther King?' . . . People don't understand that power exists within the collectivity."

"The peoples," as E.D. Nixon said.

Back at the bus, bathed in the vague and mysterious light, Joe Dickerson says, "Things are changing."

Someday they'll have that museum.

"When the time is right."

And bus No. 5726 will be waiting.

# BORN TO RUN

George Herbert Walker Bush, the 41st president of
the U.S., is today a well-respected ex-president and
the father of a second generation of towering political
figures. Yet, once upon a time, he was reviled as a whiny,
waffling, boot-licking wimp? How did it ever come to
this?

It's a 25-minute ride at a good clip on a rough ocean to the Saco
River, where George Bush has heard the bluefish are biting. Along
the way, he gives the nickel tour—how to read the wind in the
whitecaps, the island where he picnicked as a boy, the boulders
hidden beneath the rising tide. Bush knows every rock along this
Maine coast. He has come here 61 of his 62 summers. Only getting
shot down in the Pacific kept him away in 1944. Soon he is trolling
the Saco breakwater, fighting tangled lines and back-lashed reels
beneath cawing sea gulls swirling against a gunmetal sky. Bush leans
comfortably against the captain's chair of his 28-foot Cigarette boat,
the *Fidelity*, one hand on the wheel, the other holding his fishing rod
off the starboard side. He wears old blue cotton pants, a ratty navy-
blue pullover sweater, a camouflage cap and dirty Reeboks. And he
tells his fisherman's tale: He caught three big blues a while back over
at Wood Island Light.

Uh-huh, sure.

No, really.

George Bush is a political phenom in reverse. He has made a life of
mythic proportions seem somehow trivial, and he cannot understand
why. He was the most lovable boy, always. President of his class at
prep, president of everything else, too. Never a bad word about him.

A war hero—not like John Kennedy, but an undisputed war hero. Skull and Bones, Phi Beta Kappa at Yale. Cushy job offers up the ying-yang. George said no. He packed his wife and infant son into an old red Studebaker and hit the road for god-awful, rough-necking West Texas—and drilled a fortune in black gold. Then Congress, the U.N., China, the CIA, Saint Reagan's veep. Most Americans view him darn favorably too, according to the pollsters. So why the mean quips? "There's no there there." Why the David Letterman gag lines? Why the *Doonesbury* attack on his manhood?

How did it ever come to this: George Herbert Walker Bush reviled as a whiny, waffling, boot-licking wimp?

What I knew of George Bush a few months ago is what you know of him now—a grainy blur of telegenic biases: competent but boring, sometimes shrill, sometimes goofy, speaks high when low will do, Eastern scion hiding out in Texas, a moderate doing a Rose Mary Woods stretch to the Right. But this is TV knowledge, something akin to heat rising off a summer highway. The idea was to toss out all these vague impressions and start from scratch. What makes George run? Bush, jealous of his privacy, had his doubts. But his aides saw a chance to humanize his image, and they prevailed on him.

The door swung open for interviews with his brothers and sister, children, wife, mother, boyhood buddies, business partners and political cronies. There was a visit to his Waspy home town of Greenwich, Conn., a tour of the elegant Victorian where Bush grew up, walks along the streets of Midland, Tex., where he got rich. Finally, I was invited to Walker's Point, the Bush family compound in Maine, where Bush, his wife and their children and families were vacationing. They worshiped at St. Ann's Episcopal Church, ate hot dogs on the deck at Walker's Point, sang "Happy Birthday" to a Bush grandson. But George Bush and I also sat in the old care-taker's cottage and talked about what I had learned of his life and its two recurring themes—great ability and great privilege. Bush is magical—smart, funny, charming—and I found myself wanting him to like me. Intimacy is his gift. But let's face it: Bush was handed opportunity after opportunity because of his family's wealth and influence, making him also a child of a lasting American inequality.

As a boy, Bush wanted to be president, and his rare mix of ability and privilege has given him a shot.

Let me tell you, the vice president of the United States is very tired of hearing this. When I return to Walker's Point later that day for a fishing trip, Bush's wife, Barbara, pulls me aside. George had come back from the caretaker's cottage and said Barbara shouldn't be surprised if the boat returned one person lighter. I'm sure he was joking. But imagine his distress. One more story calling him just another rich man's kid. This story doesn't say that, but Bush couldn't have known that then. And as George Bush, his 40-year-old son George Jr. and I bob lazily on the Saco River, the vice president becomes suddenly reflective.

"I think you think 'class' is more important than I do," he says.

I suggest—I'm smiling when I say this—that people at the bottom of society often think social class is more important than do people at the top. But Bush will not be deterred. What did I mean when I said he was a product of America's upper class? Bush believes "class" is the snottiness and arrogance found in some rich people, those who think they are "better" than the less well-off. He says he has never felt that way. Exactly what does the word "class" mean to me?

This is an uncomfortable turning of the reportorial tables, and I am less than eloquent. But in fits and starts I say that "social class" is all about family connections and money and expectations and training, and what those can mean. I say the sons of fathers in high-level jobs end up in high-level jobs about half the time, while the sons of manual workers end up in high-level jobs about 20 percent of the time. I say that social class shapes everything from our self-esteem to our child-rearing to our sense of control over our lives. I say that education is the great American leveler—but that rich kids get more of it. And that families like the Bushes often send their kids to expensive private schools to ensure their leg up.

This sounds, well, un-American to George Jr., and he rages that it is crap from the '60s. Nobody thinks that way anymore! But his father cuts him off. "No, I want to understand what he's saying." He seems genuinely interested—and relieved that I don't plan to call him snotty. But the amazing thing is that Bush finds these ideas so novel. He seems baffled that I could see America in this way. People who work the hardest—even though some have a head start—will usually get ahead, he says. To see it otherwise is divisive.

I confess: I think a lot of Americans see it otherwise.

No matter, the secret to what makes George Bush tick is not philosophical. It is somewhere here at Walker's Point, a boot of rocky land jutting austerely into the Atlantic. The place has been in the family since 1899, and it's home to the Bush family values. The Bushes are big on values. They exude them, impose them on each other and themselves, use them to judge friend and foe. And in his grandfatherly role, George Bush has become the keeper of these values.

A few years ago, for instance, he wrote a letter to his oldest grandson, George Prescott, who was then 6. It is a surprising letter, surprising for its warmth and for its nostalgic recall—traits not associated with Bush's sometimes graceless persona. Yet the letter also evokes the Bush family expectations for the next generation, the generation in training. The letter consciously binds young George Prescott's very senses to the family, past and present, and to the objects that surround him at Walker's Point, as they did his father, his grandfather, his great-grandfather. It transforms these objects— a rock, a boat, a great-grandparent—into talismans for the family values of tradition, empathy and loyalty. It's not a letter meant for a boy, but a letter meant to be read again and again as the boy becomes a man.

"Dear 'P' " the letter begins, to distinguish the child from the vice president and George Jr. (In the Bush family, everyone seems to be named after everyone else in the family.)

"I've been thinking a lot about this summer. I had a very good time. . . . It was fun going out in the *Fidelity*—remember the day we caught all those greasy pollock. . . . That was a good day. . . . You and Noelle liked the Beach a lot, but I don't like going there. Now I am too old for that. If I get cold I get all stiff, just like my own Dad used to do. . . . This year for the first time I felt a little that way. . . . Another thing that was fun for me but wasn't too much fun for you and Noelle. It was when we went over to see My Mother—'Ganny to your Dad and Mom, Great Ganny to you.' I loved checking up on her—wasn't she nice? She always cares how the other guy feels.

"But, 'P', I've been thinking about it a lot—the most fun was the big rock boat, climbing out on it. . . . Watching you and Noelle playing on it. Near the end of the summer when the moon was full the tides were higher, and there was that special day at high tide when it almost seemed like the boat was real. . . .

"No, I think the most fun was that rock boat. . . . Don't ask me why this was the most fun. Maybe it's cause just at that moment I turned a corner in my life. I could see down the road with no fear and I suddenly had great happiness because I felt that in 50 years or so, you'd be there out on that rock boat—loving the ocean as I do, surrounded by family love—aching a little bit when it gets cold. I can't wait til next summer—Love, Gampy."

This is what makes George run. It was bred in his bones.

*"It was a, uh, very enjoyable, a very un-noteworthy existence. We were very lucky."*

*— George Bush, on his childhood*

The house on Grove Lane had no number when George Bush was a boy. People just called it the Bush house, and everyone in Greenwich knew. The town, about 45 minutes from Manhattan via the New Haven train line, was among the wealthiest communities in America. With its endless miles of stone fences and homes visible from the road only when the leaves were off the trees, Greenwich was the proverbial world apart. Its great summer estates, those of the Rockefellers and the Milbanks, had been subdivided by the '30s, but the bankers, brokers and businessmen who bought Greenwich's new miniature estates assured its affluence. The Great Depression raged, but the children of Greenwich would grow up without even a memory of it.

"Did you talk about the issues of privilege versus underprivilege, the haves and the have-nots?" George Bush's younger brother Jonathan is asked.

"No, no, no," he answers.

George Bush attended the private Greenwich Country Day School in his elementary years. It was the kind of place where students could joke about how their chauffeurs had gotten them to school on time during even the worst of blizzards. The Bush chauffeur, Alec, was among the best. At home, there were maids and a cook, golf and tennis lessons, the whole nine yards. Christmases were spent in South Carolina, where Mrs. Bush's father, George Herbert Walker, owned a plantation named Duncannon. On their visits, the children awoke in the freezing mornings to the sound of the Black servants building crackling pine fires in their bedrooms.

With the hot months of summer, the Bushes left Greenwich for Maine, where Grandfather Walker also owned Walker's Point. The Walker family, in the dry goods business in St. Louis, had bought the place to escape the summer polio epidemics of the city. George's father, Prescott Bush, a New York financier, would arrive in Maine by sleeper car on Saturday mornings and return Sunday nights. The children had a small motorboat, and the neighbor kids always marveled that George and his older brother, Pressy, were allowed to take it out alone.

"There wasn't much 'heavy weather' in those days," recalls FitzGerald Bemiss, an old George Bush friend from the years their families summered together in Maine. George and his friends—the children of other white, rich and successful fathers—fished and swam and heaved ripe rose hips at each other along the rocky waterfront. And at night, George and Pressy climbed into their bunk beds on the screened-in porch and fell asleep to the sound of the pounding surf.

If all this sounds a little Old Worldly, it was. George's mother, Dorothy Walker Bush, 85 and still living in Greenwich, chuckles self-consciously at the memory, especially the thought of George and Pressy being driven to school by Alec the chauffeur. "It seems unbelievable now," she laughs.

Yet all this gentility harbored a fierce competitiveness. Grandfather Walker, after whom George Bush is named, was a champion polo player and the donor of golf's Walker Cup British-American amateur competition. Grandfather Bush was a fine golfer and George's father was the Yale baseball team captain and Ohio's amateur golf champion. Mrs. Bush's brother, Herbert, called Uncle Herbie in the family, was an avid golfer and a Yale letterman in baseball. Prescott and Herbie, the reigning family patriarchs, were fierce competitors, and a guest on the golf course was once shocked to see a virulent argument break out between them when the guest declared a 10-inch Prescott putt a "gimmie."

"You can't give him that putt!" Herbie fumed. The guest didn't.

George's mother was competitive, too, but delightfully so. A superb golfer and tennis player, she never lost her temper at a bad shot or a muffed putt or criticized poor play in others. Her young sons might be storming around the court, throwing tennis rackets, kicking the net, but she would ignore them, and calmly call out the score. Dorothy Bush was a lithe, beautiful, vivacious woman with a marvelous sense of humor. A devout Episcopalian, she seemed to live by the Bible's pieties effortlessly. "I didn't ever say anything disagreeable about anyone in front of her," recalls FitzGerald Bemiss. Behind her gentleness, though, Mrs. Bush also took her games seriously. Visitors discovered, for instance, that she wouldn't pair them with their spouses at say, tennis, unless the couple was well-matched. Feckless adult athletes found themselves playing children.

The Bushes competed at everything—golf, tennis, tiddlywinks, backgammon, blackjack, bridge, anagrams. Anything that measured one person against another. When George was a young man, his teen-age brother, nicknamed Bucky, was given a new ball-in-a-labyrinth game and beat George handily. Bucky went to bed proud and awoke to George's casual challenge to a rematch. George won with a perfect score. Family members, in on the joke, howled with laughter: George had stayed up late perfecting his game to ambush Bucky.

Yet the competitiveness remained good-natured. The concept of "family" was so powerful that it sometimes seemed to friends that the Bush children functioned as a single mind rather than as five kids fighting for parental affection. No doubt some of that grew from a unique quirk of Mrs. Bush's, who tempered her children's hell-bent, prideful pursuit of victory with this ironclad rule: No one could brag! "I just couldn't bear braggadocio," she says.

The Bush kids did not automatically get respect; they earned it. George Bush's son Jeb, 33, would later say that he and his siblings believed they "weren't crap" until they'd gone out and proven themselves on their own. Says George Bush: "That's exactly the way I felt 40 years ago." Bush is terrible at recalling childhood stories, but one sticks clearly in his mind. At 8 years old he came home from tennis and told his mom he'd been "off his game." With uncharacteristic anger, she snapped, "You don't have a game! Get out and work harder and maybe someday you will."

"You just didn't talk about yourself," recalls Jonathan Bush. "Bad taste."

Aimed at shaping humility in proud, rich children who could easily come to think they were "better" than others, this attitude kept the Bush kids from acting self-important. Yet there's also a tension between craving recognition and enforced humility. "These people regarded themselves as 'better,' " Nicholas King, author of a sympathetic 1980 Bush biography, says of New England's patrician class. "Bush has neutralized this. But at one time he would have had to be this way." Indeed, Bush's inbred reluctance to "blow on" about himself now seems constantly at war with his prideful craving for admiration.

"You could never come home and say you played well in a game," Jonathan Bush says. "I think it was a mistake, frankly. . . . You're really suppressing your joy in achievement." The result: Pressy could brag that George had played well or George could brag that Pressy had played well. A child could bask in success only through the eyes of admirers. At this, George became the master. All the Bushes liked the limelight, says Bush's boyhood friend George de B. Bell, whose family also summered in Maine, but George liked it the most. "He wanted to be the Number 1 guy," Bell says. "It was in his makeup." With George's father around, that was difficult. He was an imposing 6 feet 4, a stiff, stern man, gracious and friendly, but formal even with his children. "At one point I said I never heard him fart," says Jonathan Bush, laughing. You'd never find Prescott on his knees giving horsey-back rides or putting together a toy train set. He rarely joined the family games, which seemed to swirl around him. And he was very sparing in his praise.

"You might get a note at school," George Bush recalls.

"And what would he say?"

" 'I was very proud to see that you were elected captain of the team.' "

"How would he sign it?"

"Devotedly, Dad."

Prescott Bush had gone to private high school in Newport, R.I., then to Yale, where he was inducted into the prestigious secret society Skull and Bones, a direct pipeline to America's Eastern Establishment. At Yale, Prescott became friends with E. Roland Harriman. A few years out of college, Prescott married Dorothy Walker, whose father had left his finance firm in St. Louis to head a Wall Street investment firm being started by Roland Harriman's brother, Averell, who eventually became the quintessential member of the Eastern Establishment—financier, ambassador and adviser to presidents. Prescott Bush followed his father-in-law to the firm that eventually became Brown Brothers Harriman.

Despite these powerful connections, Bush family folklore held that Prescott's own father had given him only $300 after college, which meant Prescott was a self-made man. Prescott worked long hours. He was forever taking important calls in his study. He was a Greenwich hospital board member and for 20 years served in the Greenwich government. He was home only a few nights a week. On Saturdays, he played golf.

"We were all terrified of him as boys," says Jonathan Bush.

The kids never knew it, Mrs. Bush says, but Prescott wanted to enter politics as a young man. He didn't enjoy business much and rarely talked about it—he talked politics. He believed, however, that he first had to put his five children through their de rigueur private educations, elementary through college—costing literally hundreds of thousands of dollars even then. So he was 57 before he became a U.S. senator; 67 when he retired in failing health. With pride and sadness, Mrs. Bush hints at a failed ambition: "He would have been the president of the United States if he'd gone into politics earlier."

Prescott Bush became the family's idealized image of achievement, propriety and duty. He talked constantly of the need to "give something back" to the society that had treated him so well. And if the Walker side of the family contributed its fun-loving spirit to the family, it was Prescott who contributed its stoic sense of noblesse oblige.

In personality, though, George took after his ebullient and empathetic mother. He liked pleasing people, and it was often said that he'd someday become a minister. "He was the easiest child to bring up, very obedient," says Mrs. Bush. She and George were great friends, sometimes even getting under the skin of the stiff-necked Prescott. George and his mother often broke into giggles at Sunday service, earning Father's glare. She also told the children that when Prescott joined the Elks, he sat naked on a huge cake of ice as his initiation. The idea of Father naked on a cake of ice put them in stitches—if Father wasn't around. Says Jonathan: "Dad was no laughing matter."

Yet George rarely got in trouble with Dad, skirting the edge of his temper so that Prescott had to chuckle. Even then, George's intuition was sharp, and everyone came to recognize his magic. Young George was like a laboratory clone of his mother's personality and his father's values. He acquired his father's ambition but also his mother's enchantment. He was so kind, always watching out for the fat kid who couldn't keep up. He was the most popular boy with the kids—and with the grown-ups.

"He was earmarked in the family as a tremendous winner," says Uncle Herbie's son, George Herbert Walker III. Uncle Herbie—19 years older and a powerful, successful man himself—idolized young George. He believed George could do anything, and later would show that confidence in the form of half a million dollars in investor financing for George, the young oil man.

By the time Bush was ready for high school, his father wanted him out of the stilted atmosphere of Greenwich. He picked Phillips Academy, called Andover after the Massachusetts town where it's located. Old and prestigious, Andover emphasized not only social pedigree but merit. Even then, it admitted a handful of Blacks and Jews and had a large number of scholarship students. So despite its securely elitist cast, Andover was a place where kids could learn, as Prescott said, "to mix with everybody."

At Andover, George excelled again. His senior yearbook entry lists more activities than any classmate—student council secretary, senior class president, captain of the soccer and baseball teams, and 20 others. Bush's grades were mediocre, but he was, if not the most popular boy at Andover, certainly among them. And classmate Walter J.P. Curley voices what was by then a refrain: "George was a star." At Andover, classmates also began saying something else about George Bush: They began saying he would be president of the United States someday.

*I had a very powerful father. . . . Very much of a leader and admired by everybody, and I didn't want to do something on his, I had a kind of a, not a competitive thing with him, but I wanted to go out and do something on my own.*

Secretary of War Henry L. Stimson must have made a lot of parents breathe easier when he told the members of the 1942 Andover graduating class they shouldn't enlist in World War II, but go on to college. Most boys listened. Not George Bush.

"Has this changed your idea?" Mrs. Bush asked George as they walked out of Cochran Chapel after Stimson's speech.

"Not a bit!" George responded.

Mrs. Bush had already tried to talk her son out of enlisting, without luck. His father too had wanted him to stay out of the war until he was drafted, but in his stiff-upper-lip manner had said nothing of his fears to George, who enlisted. He became the war's youngest Navy pilot and flew Avenger bombers in the Pacific. His plane was hit. With smoke and flames pouring from his engine, Bush still dropped his 500-pound bombs on an enemy radio station before bailing out into the ocean. His two-man crew was killed. After hours at sea, Bush, sick and vomiting, was saved from Japanese gunboats by a U.S. submarine. He was a bona fide hero, the recipient of the Distinguished Flying Cross. He would rack up 1,228 hours in the air and 58 combat missions. Yet the question remains: Why did he enlist so soon? Probably because he'd taken to heart the values of loyalty and patriotism taught by his era, his class, his father and Andover. But he also had his own reasons.

George lived in awe of his father and wondered whether he could equal his dad's record at Yale, one of Bush's Andover friends, Ernest D. Obermeyer, told Bush biographer Nicholas King. Obermeyer has since died, but King's notes show that Obermeyer believed Bush wanted "out from under" the shadow of his family. By going to war, Bush found a solution—and his way in the world. Over and over, Bush would seek his identity in doing what wasn't expected. The road led to the same place—great success. But it got him "out from under"—and assured the glory of his youth: Bush was a star. And stars do more. Bush is asked: "Was it a shock to go off to war from your background?"

He answers: "It was the shock."

George Bush still remembers his anxiety as his father put him on the train to war a month after his 18th birthday. He worried about what was by then his psychological signature: "I guess I was thinking, 'Will I be accepted?' " Bush says he was apprehensive because he was younger than most of the men. But it's hard to believe he didn't also wonder about a more ageless gap between men: Bush had never really stepped outside his insular world.

Pilot Jack Guy, for instance, was a country boy from Claxton, Ga. When Bush once mentioned that he'd gone to Andover, Jack Guy's reply was: "Well, I went to Claxton!" As ever, war is the ultimate leveler, a meritocracy where lineage takes a back seat to 20-20 vision. Says Bush, "It was a revelation." Bush was knock-down handsome then—tall, wiry, athletic—with a devil-may-care aviator style. Only the white scarf was missing. In photos from those days his angular face, clear eyes, and open smile are like a beacon. "He was a lot of fun, a live wire," recalls Guy. "Everybody wanted to cotton up to him. . . . I don't know anyone who didn't like him for any reason. I don't know how to say it any other way."

Bush was, to use the day's slang, a straight arrow, and engaged to Barbara Pierce, daughter of the Rye, N.Y., chairman of the McCall's publishing empire. "We'd go out partyin' and raise hell," remembers

Guy. "But not George. He had Barbara. Pick up gals? Not George." Bush's brother Jonathan once made this joke about why George was so dedicated to Barbara (though its insight into Bush's personality goes beyond light humor): "She was wild about him. And for George, if anyone wants to be wild about him, it's fine with him."

Though Bush was younger, he seemed more mature than the other men. He was relaxed with superior officers in a way his buddies weren't. And he was more serious. When the war ended, and everybody went out to celebrate, George and Barbara were late—their first VJ Day celebration had been at church.

"If one of us had to be great someday, it would have been George," says Bush war buddy Lou J. Grab. "He had a better education, a little more going for him." And Bush seemed to know clearly what he was fighting for. When the men went home with him on leave, they learned what some of those things were.

"What came across was when I went by his grandfather's or uncle's apartment in Manhattan," recalls Guy. "It was about the grandest thing I'd ever seen." Pilot Milton Moore, Bush's best friend in those days, was invited to Greenwich for George's wedding in '45. "I was very impressed," says Moore, whose father owned a laundry. Everybody was friendly, but Moore noticed that the young people at the wedding seemed more self-assured than those he knew. No one in Moore's family had even gone to college, but everyone there seemed to talk about college constantly. When introduced, people's colleges were added like extra last names. But Moore always felt comfortable with George. He visited Bush after the war at Yale, and he visited him later in Texas.

"Everybody liked him," says Grab. "And those qualities endured over the next 10 or even 20 years. Your attitude might have changed about some people you liked. But George endured."

*And when we hit that new century, I want the young people just starting out as we did to still have that same kind of opportunity, the same kind of opportunity that Barbara Bush and I had. And we can see that they get it.*

George Bush will not keep this promise. He can't. The opportunities that came to him do not come to the average man.

After the war, he whizzed through Yale in 2 1/2 years. He was Phi Beta Kappa, captain of the baseball team, all-around BMOC. But the greatest hint of Bush's future success came on Yale's April "tap night," when the school's best and brightest are inducted into Yale's secret societies. Bush was "the last man tapped." In tapdom's neo-Masonic world of mysterious chants and psychosexual confessions, the first are last, making Bush the most desirable man in his class. The selection might not have been a total surprise, since Bush's father and Averell Harriman were Bonesmen. But it was no small honor. Besides Harriman, Bones alums include Stimson, William Howard Taft, Henry Luce and McGeorge Bundy, to name a few.

After Yale, greatness was assumed for Bush. His cousin, George Herbert Walker III, predicted to Barbara Bush that George would be president someday. Jonathan Bush had told his prep school classmates the same thing. By then, even George had succumbed to this acclamation. Yale classmate Ethan Shepley Jr. remembers hearing at Yale that Bush planned to make money in business and then enter politics.

Brown Brothers Harriman, where his father worked, waived its nepotism rule to offer Bush a job, but he said no. He wanted "out from under." But in Bush's world it was hard to escape the womb of privilege. One of his father's closest friends, Neil Henry Mallon, was president of Dresser Industries, an oil conglomerate, and Prescott was on its board. Mallon had no children, and George was like a surrogate son. (Bush would eventually name a son after Mallon.) So when Mallon offered him a job selling oil rig equipment in Odessa, Tex., Bush took it. Here the official story of Bush's life gets embossed to fit a more Middle American model: The red Studebaker is packed with wife and baby, and off they trek.

The truth is less prosaic, but in its own way uniquely American. Bill Nelson was a hardened Texas oil-field worker, and when Bush walked into the West Texas office of the International Derrick and Equipment Co. in the summer of '48, Nelson took one look and figured he'd last a week. Bush was dressed for West Texas all right—wool trousers, white shirt, black shoes, no tie. But his manner gave him away. "He was so different from the ordinary man in West Texas," says the 88-year-old Nelson, an Ideco supervisor then. "You'd wonder, 'Why did he come out here?'"

Nelson had already been told that Bush was a Dresser board member's kid. "That meant put him to work and learn him what I could," he says. That turned out to be easy. Bush asked questions until Nelson was tired of answering them, and he worked constantly. Nelson would go home with a list of things to do atop his desk—and the next day George would already have done them. Over the years Nelson had hundreds of trainees. "George was better than any," he says.

When Bush hit town, West Texas was in the midst of the great Scurry County oil boom. Housing was so scarce in Midland and Odessa, the area's twin towns, that tent cities cropped up. The Bushes lived in Odessa, the blue-collar sister city to the white-collar Midland. Their shotgun apartment on a dirt road shared a bathroom with a whore next door. Their life seemed true-grit American— another young couple "just starting out." But their mindset was still that of the children of privilege. This foray into the workaday world was, as Barbara Bush said, an adventure. The prostitute might be staying in the shotgun digs in Odessa, but the Bushes would be moving on. It's difficult to overestimate the importance of knowing this: Real power to shape the future breeds optimism, which breeds effort, which breeds success.

"I never thought we'd live on East Seventh Street the rest of our lives," Barbara says. "I mean, trust me. . . . George and I never thought we were poor. We knew we weren't. We knew if something terrible happened to us, we had family. . . . It's a little bit smug to say these things didn't matter."

Bush hadn't set out to make a wildcatter's fortune, but he caught the fever. And he wasn't the only Eastern import who did; they were swarming all over the place. Dubbed the "Ivy Leaguers," these migrants became key players in West Texas oil. The imports weren't all Ivy Leaguers, but one quality distinguished many of them: They too were from well-connected families of wealth and privilege. Even wildcatting wasn't an equal opportunity employer.

Bush arrived at just the right time for his rare blend of ability and privilege. Before World War II, wildcatting was a mom-and-pop store. But rising drilling costs had made financing tougher. Bush and the Ivy Leaguers brought what the natives needed: pipelines to money. "Connections were the whole game," says C. Fred Chambers, a Texas oil man who became Bush's best friend.

Independent oil men are oil-deal promoters who convince landowners to sell a portion of their mineral rights to investors. In return, the promoter gets a free share of the deal. Bush did this successfully and then with William C. and J. Hugh Liedtke, who would later form Pennzoil, he created Zapata Petroleum. The Liedtkes, whose father was Gulf Oil's chief legal counsel in Tulsa, had gone to private high school and Amherst College. They tapped their Tulsa connections for about half-a-million dollars and Bush tapped his Eastern connections for the same—with the help of his admiring Uncle Herbie's investor clients. Zapata scored: 128 wells without a dry hole.

In oil deals over the years, Bush would hit on his Eastern connections again and again. Fred Chambers, whose connections were modest compared with Bush's, recalls with awe a meeting he and Bush had with Eugene Meyer, a founder of Allied Chemical Corp., the principal owner of the *Washington Post* and a friend of Prescott Bush.

"Well, how'd we do on those other deals, George?" Meyer asked.

"Pretty well," Bush said.

With that, Meyer invested $50,000. He then offered the young men a ride to the train station, and as they were leaving his limousine, Meyer asked: "Say, do you have any more of that deal?" Bush said yes—and Meyer invested another $25,000. Such was Bush's world. At 30, he already traveled in circles that hard work, charm, brains and empathy alone could never have opened.

In Midland, as usual, Bush was being everything to everybody. His wife recalls that so many people depended on him then that she was jealous. He coached boys' baseball, helped found the YMCA and the community theater, and was a director of a new Midland bank. Again, the two threads: "He did represent some outside financial interests from New York and Tulsa," says Midland oil man Earle M. Craig Jr. "But he wouldn't have been asked if he weren't an outstanding young man."

In '52, Bush got into politics, opposing the old Robert A. Taft Republicans in Texas in favor of Dwight D. Eisenhower. Back in Connecticut, his father was doing the same as part of a group that talked Ike into running for president. Once a staunch Herbert Hoover man, Prescott Bush was at the heart of the Republican Party's shift away from old-line conservatism toward a more non-ideological, pragmatic Republicanism that had made its peace with the New Deal. In '52, he was elected to the U.S. Senate. He mixed well with the beer-hall crowds, but wasn't totally at ease.

"I always thought Pres did a very good job of mingling with the ordinary guy, but he really didn't understand them very well," says John Alsop, a Republican mover in Connecticut for the past 40 years. "He'd just never been one."

By the mid-'50s George Bush would tell his closest friend, Fred Chambers, that he hoped to enter politics someday. It was a good choice, a way to earn the prideful affirmation and boundless admiration he craved at the same time he could humbly "give something back." He also pushed ahead in business, moving to Houston and forming Zapata Off-Shore, one of the nation's first offshore oil-drilling companies. It was a tough business. Zapata prospered modestly; Bush got a bleeding ulcer. Meanwhile, Prescott Bush was having the time of his life in the Senate. He loved politics and believed George would too. Harry Hurt III, writing in *Texas Monthly* magazine, reported this 1961 exchange between Prescott and Houston Republican James A. Bertron:

Prescott: "Jimmy, when are you going to get George involved?"

Bertron: "Senator, I'm trying. We're all trying."

*What I hope people perceive is reasonableness.*

George Bush finally did it in '64—ran for the U.S. Senate in Texas. Most of his business friends were baffled about why he wanted to give up a fortune, sacrifice the privacy, take all the crap.

"You know, I just love it!" Bush told a friend. If Bush had 10 minutes between campaign speeches, he was out shaking hands. On the road, he was up at 6 a.m. delivering coffee to his staffers' rooms. "I think he is very uncomfortable without people around," says Chase Untermeyer, a Bush friend and campaign worker from those days. "He craves people."

Bush's political philosophy through two races for the U.S. Senate and a single contested race for Congress was, like his father's, a pragmatic, eminently reasonable conservatism. He ran as a Goldwater Republican in '64, but by Texas standards he was a moderate. He took way-out liberal positions such as opposing repeal of the federal income tax. Yet he was a hawk on Vietnam and an opponent of civil rights legislation. He called Robert F. Kennedy "a left-wing carpetbagger" and Medicare "socialized medicine." He lost. In '66, Bush was elected to Congress from a safe, silk-stocking Republican district in Houston and his views became more liberal. He voted for civil rights legislation, the 18-year-old vote, the abolition of the draft. He backed a call for American withdrawal from Vietnam. According to Americans for Constitutional Action, a conservative ratings group, Bush's voting record fell from 83 percent conservative in 1967 to 58 percent conservative in 1970.

"At that time he told me he regretted having gone that far right and that he'd never do it again," recalls the Rev. John F. Stevens, the former secretary of the Executive Council of the U.S. Episcopal Church. "The implication was he had to do it to get elected."

The pragmatic Bush was a hot political property. His ability was respected in Congress, and as a first-term member he was given the rare honor of a seat on the House Ways and Means Committee. But the other great force was also at work. "His father came to me . . . and wanted him on my committee," recalls Wilbur D. Mills, then Democratic chairman of Ways and Means and an old friend of Prescott Bush. "I said, 'I'm a Democrat and I don't think I can do anything.' He said, could I call Jerry Ford? And so I did." Ford was then Republican leader of the House. "He engineered that," Mills says, as a favor to Prescott Bush. Ford recalls helping Bush win the seat, but as a way to give Texas Republicans "a shot in the arm." He says, however, that Bush wouldn't have gotten it if Mills had objected.

But Bush had a higher calling: As a congressman, he told Houston minister Hartsell Gray that after meeting the men who ran Washington, Bush knew he could handle any job in town. "That included the presidency," says Gray.

"It was the same drive to do something on his own that got him down to Texas," Bush friend Ernest Obermeyer told biographer Nicholas King. "A driving sense of accomplishment. Once he has accomplishment, he has a tendency to walk away from it. . . . His attitude was, 'Well, I've done that. And that wasn't so hard. And let's see what I can do next. . . . ' He wasn't willing to wait around. He was after the ultimate challenge—first the Senate and then the presidency."

In pursuit of his great ambition, Bush ran for the Senate in '70 and lost. He stayed in politics by taking an appointment as the U.S. ambassador to the United Nations, then as the U.S. liaison in China and then as the director of the CIA. In '80, these jobs would justify Bush's run for the White House. His slogan: "A president we won't have to train." In truth, the years of broad experience were epilogue to a life's ambition.

"When did you decide to run for president?" *New Yorker* magazine reporter Elizabeth Drew asked Bush in 1980.

"Well," Bush replied. "I started thinking a long time ago—I mean, like, hasn't everybody thought about being president for years?"

*It's just plain beautiful. And it's ours. It's our piece of turf.*

After four hours of trolling the Saco River, George Bush finally gives up. No vice presidential fish fry tonight. But it has turned out to be a glorious afternoon, the wind about 18 knots, the sky clearing, the sea beautifully rugged. Bush quotes someone who once said that the time a man spends fishing shouldn't count toward the time God allotted that man on earth. He says this several times, so I figure he wants to be quoted. That's okay. It's a good line. Because in all my hours with Bush these are the first I feel relaxed. Private time with him is indeed magical. It's a nice feeling to have about a man who would be president. But does it really matter?

Well, it matters in one way. They say George Bush doesn't know himself, that he has blown with the political winds: Goldwater conservative to Jerry Ford conservative to Ronald Reagan conservative. This is silly. George Bush knows exactly who he is: He is the son of Sen. Prescott Bush, the son of Dorothy Walker Bush. He is a Bush, a ragingly proud Bush. He was in a very real sense born to rule. And when you are born to rule, you rule what there is to rule. He didn't come to this ambition by ideology, but by osmosis. Bush wants to be president, always has. And he is a reasonable man. He'll change with the times—and change back with them again. He opposed civil rights legislation, then favored it. He backed the Vietnam war, but later wanted American soldiers withdrawn. He opposed a constitutional amendment barring most legal abortions, but now favors such an amendment. He opposed Ronald Reaganism, but he now favors it.

Issues don't motivate Bush; people and ambition motivate him. His ardent backers spout not ideology, but faith in his goodness. Wasn't it reasonable to oppose civil rights legislation in '64, reasonable to favor it in '68? Remember, Bush's father was a Hoover man who helped draft Ike. Changing with the times, a guiltless pragmatism, is Bush's trademark. He is a living barometer of the middle course.

Bush's personality—his reasonableness, his decency, his empathy—is the glue of his politics. Oddly enough, they also explain how so mythic a life can seem somehow trivial. George Bush has never been immutably tied to the great currents of his time. He's no trailblazer. His political motives aren't as much linked to a special vision of the body politic as they are to his family's dedication to proving itself again and again. The presidency, as Ernest Obermeyer said, is Bush's ultimate challenge, the final affirmation. This isn't a flaw in his character. It is the heart of his character.

A key to understanding Bush is his belief that he can make almost everyone happy. While Bush is on the *Fidelity*, a man flicks him the bird from shore. Barbara is along, and she teases that George should turn around and go talk to the man, win him over. Husband and wife banter and laugh. But deep down, I bet they believe George could win that man over. It is his gift.

But Bush isn't built for TV. He's hot while the medium is cool. He sometimes seems on fire, out of control on TV, his metallic voice screeching like chalk on a blackboard. In person, the uncertain, melodic quiver, the breaks in pitch, the halting sentences, the fragments of thought, aren't grating. In person, his manner evokes a natural intimacy, like the fumbling, boyish eloquence of Jimmy Stewart. On TV, he can seem weak and confused. The natural tension between Bush's enforced humility and his great pride can, under hostile questioning, also surface in flashes of temper.

"I don't suffer fools in the questioning area gladly," Bush says. Then, as if hearing Mother's admonition, he adds, "I'm doing better now."

Yet another message that Bush sends is subliminal. It's the message he can't help but send, the one in which his lineage traps him, the other edge to the sword of privilege. Nothing irks Bush more than the harping about his "preppy" style. He has abandoned button-down collars, half-rimmed glasses, even his striped watchband—something he swore he'd never do—to shed the image. It's all pettiness to him. But there's more going on here. These are totems that remind Americans that Bush is of a world apart. He can preach a renewed American opportunity, equal opportunity, but his life is testament to what can happen when one boy is more equal than others. This doesn't diminish his achievements. God knows there were others who did less with more. Truth is, Bush left the oil business for politics just before oil went gangbusters. He's worth a modest $2 million today, and he occasionally wonders about the fortune left behind.

But in politics, Bush's image must filter through a have-not American knowledge that Bush, for all his empathy, can little understand. So many men have worked for the boss' son, competent or not. So many women have watched men climb the males-only ladder. So many Blacks, ethnics and blue-collar kids have seen competency include social skills acquired not by hard work or brains but by birth, breeding and education. Why is Bush's ebullient optimism the butt of jokes? Maybe because many people can't share his joy in the American experience.

These aren't hard data. They are biases. To be honest, they are my biases. But am I alone? Is it an accident that Americans have elected only one president born to the upper class since Franklin Roosevelt? And that was John Kennedy—a rich kid with the instincts of a rogue Irishman. What I wanted from Bush was an admission, some acknowledgment that on the simplest human level the privileges in his life were unfair. Bush simply doesn't agree with this. Or he can't acknowledge it.

"Any society, any capitalistic society, is gonna have some people who are well-to-do and some who are not doing very well, and who are poor. Abjectly poor. . . . What you do is try to strive hard [so] that it's as equal as possible. And you gotta recognize that sometimes there are, even in a system as good as ours, certain inequities. . . . In other words, you're looking at the glass half empty, I'm looking at it half full." Of his background, Bush says, "I view it, as you know, with great pride. And no sense of wanting to cooperate by saying, 'Gosh, isn't it awful that my, you know, family were privileged. . . . ' So I'm not apologetic. So long as I make a contribution and my kids do."

George Bush is without social guilt, which is probably good for his mental health. He struggled admirably to justify his great privilege—as do many children of successful parents—and in his mind, he has proven his worth beyond all doubt. "You don't think I could have made it, made something of myself?" he asks wearily. There's a plaintiveness to that question, and, frankly, Bush has earned his identity as a member of the deserving rich. But looking at America from the bottom up, doesn't it also seem naive to believe that Bush, if born to a wholly different world, would be vice president today? Hearing Bush preach the American Gospel—no matter how much I like him—is still like listening to a very tall man praise the virtues of being very tall. I think: Yeah, that's easy for you to say.

And I think of what John Alsop said of Bush's father. "I always thought Pres did a very good job of mingling with the ordinary guy, but he really didn't understand them very well. He'd just never been one."

They say George Bush is most like himself when he's at Walker's Point. He loves to fish for a while, then roar off with his twin Mercruisers at full throttle, his boat flying into the air over the mountainous swells as he spins the *Fidelity* 180 degrees to a quick stop, and then fish some more. In the summers, the Bush children visit Walker's Point with their kids. They're all married, the boys successful businessmen. There has never been a divorce in the Bush family. The kids work in charities. One son mans a soup line at Christmas. Bush's son Marvin, 30, says they are spared the social guilt so many rich kids suffer because they learned to give something back.

"It's a base for family," George Bush says of Walker's Point. "And it's the setting that somehow relieves all tensions and frees you up to think. . . . I love to go out in the sea when it's rough. I like to stay out on the rocks with my grandchildren. . . . It frees up your soul. . . . And a lot of it's 'cause it has memories."

Walker's Point is what it's all about for George Bush. The main house was wiped out in a flood in '78, and Bush had the place rebuilt. He uses Walker's Point as his "anchor to windward." So do his children. So will his grandchildren.

Bush slouches comfortably in a chair on the back deck. It's a sunny day, the waves crash on the rocks a hundred feet away and little George Prescott, now 10, climbs alone on the huge rock boat between Bush and the sea. Today the rock is a toy, tomorrow it will be a symbol.

The idea is that all this will be passed on. Not just the house, the educations, the connections, but the values—hard work, giving something back, the family as rock in a sand castle world. If everything goes right, little George Prescott won't feel social guilt, he'll give something back, he'll be magical, he'll keep the lineage alive. Because the Bushes are their own kind of American dynasty. And all these things will be bred in his bones.

# DUBYA AND ME

On having a long and fascinating acquaintanceship
with the 43rd president of the U.S., a man who would
become one of the most admired and, later, most reviled
presidents in U.S. history.

They still called him Junior when we first met, in forlorn Midland,
Texas, back in July 1986. He was known then for being the son
of the vice president of the United States, the agonizingly named
George Herbert Walker Bush. As a young staff writer at the
*Washington Post Magazine*, I was trying to persuade Vice President Bush
to let me spend several months with him for an in-depth profile I
intended to write. But the veep was skeptical, and he left it up to
Junior to pass judgment on me and my request.

"Come on down and visit," the man who would eventually be
known to the world as President George W. Bush drawled cheerfully
to me over the phone. "But I won't tell you any good stuff until I'm
sure you're not going to do an ax job."

So began a long and fascinating acquaintanceship with the man
who would become one of the most admired and, later, reviled presidents in U.S. history. Over the next 25 years, our paths crossed again
and again, most recently in his Dallas office last April. I had just read
Bush's 2010 memoir *Decision Points*, and I was struck by his many
references to history. In the back of my mind was an article that Karl
Rove had written for the *Wall Street Journal* in 2008, which revealed
(much to the consternation of the president's derisive critics) that
Bush had read 186 books for pleasure in the preceding three years,
consisting mostly of serious historical nonfiction. Intrigued, I asked
Bush whether he would talk to me about how his passion for reading
history had shaped his presidency and perspective, and he agreed.

When I sat down to write about that meeting, however, a different story emerged. History is composed of significant and less significant moments, the trouble being that we often don't know at the time which is text and which is footnote. Yet when it comes to presidents, even footnotes are worth recording. I realized that what I had before me was a story that went beyond politics or policies or the reading habits of a president, an idiosyncratically personal story, a footnote-to-history story spanning a quarter-century.

Midland, 1986: George W. and I met in the 13th-floor office of his oil exploration business. He looked fit, had run 10 miles the day before—his 40th birthday. An open-collared light-blue shirt, sweat rings, shadow of a beard, nice tan, handsome, macho. He tenaciously lipped an unlit cigarette, and I could feel his incendiary impatience. Even then, he broke his sentences, got them jumbled, his thoughts careening. He was blunt and indiscreet, and he made intensely disparaging off-the-record remarks about some of his father's political rivals.

George W. talked mostly about his dad, admiringly, of course. About how GHWB had been a World War II fighter pilot who, upon graduating from Yale, left the safety and comfort of the Eastern establishment for Midland and the oil works. As an aside, we also talked about W., how he, too, had gone to Yale, learned to fly fighter jets, and moved to West Texas to make it in the oil biz. He wasn't exactly bragging, but he was letting me know that he, too, was accomplished, although he seemed well aware that his life so far was one writ small compared with his dad's.

"I'm putting myself in his shoes, I guess," he said, adding that he couldn't remember when he stopped competing with his dad, but he had. With what I took as pride that his father had asked him to vet me, he said, "He trusts my judgment now."

Perhaps the operative word was "now"—finally, at age 40.

What I couldn't have known, of course, was that July 1986 would be a watershed moment in the life of George W. Bush, who was then having a running contest with too much drink. He had embarrassed his parents by asking a female dinner guest what sex was like after 50. He had cursed out a reporter in a restaurant in front of the reporter's child. Three weeks after my visit, while on a morning jog and suffering from still another hangover, W. decided to stop drinking, which he did, cold turkey.

In Midland all those years ago, the normal distance between prominent source and reporter didn't apply, and W. invited me out to a Mexican restaurant with Laura and their 4-year-old twin daughters, who got in trouble for throwing chips, were threatened with a spanking, and went home without dessert. He also invited me to his house, where I found books by John Fowles, F. Scott Fitzgerald, James Joyce and Gore Vidal lying about, as well as biographies of Willa Cather and Queen Victoria. A few years later, I might even have thought they had been purposely left there for the eyes of a reporter, but not on that unstaged evening. Laura would eventually write that even then, George read every night in bed.

I also found an open Bible in the house. "I've read it cover to cover, and it wouldn't hurt you, Walt, to do the same," Bush said, laughing. Within the last year, W. had begun a new lifetime regimen of daily Bible readings, as I and all of America would later learn.

What I remember most about my visit was Bush's personality. He was a friendly, funny, bantering, confident man, a regular guy. He was easy to like, and I liked him. More important, he also liked me and recommended that his father cooperate on my story. He even arranged for me to visit his parents at the family home in Kennebunkport, Maine, where the vice president, W. and I went fishing on his dad's famous Cigarette boat. At one point, the subject of inequality in America came up, and the vice president asked for my opinion. I said that some people were born with the leg up of money, education and connections, and that those born well-to-do often ended up doing better in life. The veep listened respectfully, but an angry W. raged on about how my view was "crap" from the '60s.

I figured that was the last I'd see of Junior.

Twenty-five years later, George W. Bush looks great. Two years as a civilian have been good to him. His feet clad in golf shoes and up on his desk, he leans back in his chair, a well-mouthed, unlit cigar as a prop. At 7:45 a.m., he's talking golf.

"I didn't play golf during my presidency except the first two years. So I came back out here, and then I decided I was going to get better at golf, not just *play* golf."

"And have you?" I ask.

"I have gotten better. The problem is I'm never good enough. That's the problem with the game. It requires discipline, patience and focus. As you know, I'm long on"—and he hesitates, smiling, losing the sentence—"well, a couple areas where I could use some improvement."

Same W.: sentences broken and jumbled, thoughts careening.

He certainly enjoys reading and talking about books. And his friends know it. On his desk is a stack of books that have come as gifts: *All Things Are Possible Through Prayer*; *Basho: The Complete Haiku*; *Children of Jihad*; and *Theodore Roosevelt's Letters to His Children*. To the pile, I add my own gift, *Cleopatra* by Pulitzer Prize-winning author Stacy Schiff. Right now, Bush is reading Ron Chernow's *Washington: A Life*, a biography of the first president. "Chernow's a great historian," Bush says excitedly. "I think one of the great history books I read was on Alexander Hamilton by Chernow. But I also read *House of Morgan*, *Titan*, and now I'm reading *Washington*."

He mentions David Halberstam's *The Coldest Winter*, a book about the Korean War that he read before a visit last year to Korea, to give a speech to evangelicals. "I stand up in front of 65,000 Christians to give a speech in South Korea . . ." he says, "and I'm thinking about the bloody [battles] fought in the Korean War." Halberstam's book—coupled with earlier readings of David McCullough's *Truman* and Robert Beisner's *Dean Acheson*, a biography of Truman's secretary of state presented to him by Bush's own secretary of state, Condoleezza Rice—gave the event deeper resonance. The decisions of the unpopular President Harry S. Truman, he realized, made it possible for a former U.S. president to speak before freely worshipping Koreans 60 years later. "So history, in this case, gave me a better understanding of the moment, and . . . put it all into context—the wonder of the moment."

I tick off a partial list of people Bush has read books about in recent years in addition to Washington, Truman and Acheson: Abraham Lincoln, Andrew Carnegie, Mark Twain, Huey Long, Lyndon Johnson, Theodore Roosevelt, Andrew Mellon, Dietrich Bonhoeffer, Ulysses S. Grant, John Quincy Adams, Genghis Khan.

"Genghis Khan?" I ask incredulously.

"I didn't know much about him. I was fascinated by him. I guess I've always been fascinated by larger-than-life figures. That's why I'm looking forward to reading *Cleopatra*. I know nothing about her. . . . But you can sit there and be absorbed by TV, let the news of the moment consume you. You can just do nothing. I choose to read as a form of relaxation. . . . Laura used to say, 'Reading is taking a journey,' and she's right."

I must remind myself: *This is the same man I met in Midland, Texas.*

As it turned out, I did see George W. soon again after the encounter on his father's Cigarette boat. After my story ran in the *Washington Post Magazine*, the vice president invited my family over to lunch and horseshoes at his official residence, on the grounds of the U.S. Naval Observatory. The vice president had actually called twice to invite us over, but on both occasions, our schedules hadn't meshed. After the second invite, George W. called my house.

"Walt, my dad is vice president of the United States," I remember him saying with a touch of irritation. "When he calls and invites you to lunch, you come to lunch."

I apologized and explained the conflicts.

"So if he invites you again, you'll come?"

"Of course."

If I had been covering politics, I wouldn't have accepted such an invitation, but since I wasn't, my editor and I saw no conflict of interest. When my wife, son, daughter and I arrived on the appointed day, George W. was also there with Laura and their daughters. At one point, while the rest of us chatted, the vice president and my toddler daughter played under the table with Millie the dog. In those days, I was far less interested in the younger Bush than in the elder, about whom I was then thinking of writing a book.

During his father's presidential campaign, W. moved to Washington, and we occasionally met for lunch at the Old Ebbitt Grill, near the White House. Probably because I wasn't a political reporter, Bush was comfortable spouting off about what he considered the bad press his father was getting, about how reporters were unfairly crucifying "a good man," as W. often described his dad. He also gently boasted of his role as his dad's watchdog on his national campaign staff. W. was certainly as smart as the next guy in Washington, but president? I never imagined it.

After GHWB was elected in 1988, I proposed my book idea to him: I would leave the *Post*, shadow him through his presidency and tell the deeply personal story of what it was like to be president of the United States. Bush was intrigued enough to call his son for advice again. At a breakfast at the Hay-Adams Hotel, across Lafayette Square from the White House, with W., National Security Advisor Brent Scowcroft and White House Counsel C. Boyden Gray in attendance, I made my pitch. Afterward, W. slapped me on the back and said, "I give you a B+, Walt."

*Tough grader*, I thought.

President Bush and I went back and forth on the book idea for the first months of his presidency before he finally decided he would not undertake the project: an embedded independent reporter would inevitably learn too many national security secrets, and perhaps a few other secrets, too. Anyway, W. and I didn't talk again during his dad's presidency. But after GHWB lost his reelection bid in 1992, my wife and I got an unexpected invitation to a White House Christmas party. That evening, the president laughed and told me that now that he was on his way out, he didn't have a long list of people he had to invite to the White House; he could invite just the people he liked. W., who had moved back to his home state and become president of the Texas Rangers baseball team, was there, and we made our quick hellos before he went off to mingle. As the evening was ending, W. pulled my wife and me aside. "Dad would like you to come up to the residence after the party," he said.

So up we went in the elevator with a Secret Service man. When we got off, the president and I fell a safe distance behind my wife, W., and First Lady Barbara Bush, allowing me to privately tell President Bush I was sorry about his defeat. A few steps into the central hall outside the Lincoln Bedroom, President Bush stopped and looked me in the eye.

"You know the worst thing about it, Walt? The embarrassment. It's just so embarrassing."

As was his way, W. was mostly angry that night, believing again that the press coverage of his father was unfair and biased. "I was a reactionary for George Bush . . ." he would later tell me. "And so the criticism of my dad was unbelievably painful."

In the spring of 1993, I was in the Dallas-Fort Worth area and called W. Laura was out of town, and he invited me to his house for dinner, where I got the news: George W. Bush was thinking about running for governor of Texas. He did, and won. He won again. He became president. Then came 9/11, Afghanistan and Iraq.

Not until 2003, with the Iraq war begun, did our paths cross again.

"So what is it about history that grabs you?" I ask.

"I'm fascinated by people," Bush says, "and a lot of history is the study of individuals making a difference. . . . I haven't really sat and tried to figure out why I was interested. All I can tell you is I have been for a long period of time."

In high school, at the Phillips Academy in Andover, Massachusetts, Bush had an American history teacher, Tom Lyons, who brought the presidency of Franklin Roosevelt and the Great Depression to life. "He made history so interesting and exciting," recalls Bush, who was no star pupil, either at Andover or at Yale, where he majored in history. One of his favorite professors at Yale, Wolfgang Leonhard, had fled Nazi Germany to the Soviet Union, only to see his mother arrested under Stalin. Leonhard defected and ended up teaching the young Bush about the horrors of Soviet-era oppression. Professors such as Leonhard created in Bush, even if he was a C+ student, a lasting impression: "what it was like to live under a society in which a few made the decisions for everybody."

"When I became more sober about life"—and Bush chuckles here—"a philosophy, a kind of clarity began to take hold. . . . I think, as I matured, the seeds that had been planted during college began to take hold. In other words, the lessons I'd learned, which fascinated me at the time, actually became part of a philosophical foundation." Bush would eventually come to describe this foundation, starkly and simply, as "the struggle between tyranny and freedom."

"When I got elected governor and president, history gave me a chance to study the decisions of my predecessors," Bush says. As governor, he read *The Raven*, by Marquis James, a biography of Sam Houston, the father of Texas statehood. "I was fascinated by the story of Houston voting against secession, and reading a description of him basically being driven out of town by angry citizens. . . . My only point is that one lesson I learned, if they're throwing garbage on Houston, arguably Texas's most famous politician—Sam Houston Elementary School, where I went to school in Midland, was named for him!—if they're throwing garbage on him, they can throw garbage on me."

Bush remained calm and confident during his tumultuous presidency. Critics saw him as delusional; defenders saw him as self-assured. Bush believes that one of the most important stage requirements of the presidency is indeed never to signal weakness or self-doubt or confusion: "One of the things you learn about great leaders is that they never project the burdens of responsibility on others." He remembers Richard Carwardine's *Lincoln: A Life of Purpose and Power* (one of 14 Lincoln biographies Bush read while he was president), which recounts the 16th president's perseverance through not only military defeat after defeat, stupefying troop casualties and public ridicule, but also the death of his son Willie and the debilitating emotional turmoil of his wife.

"You're not the only person that's ever gone through hard things," Bush says of the lessons he has learned from history. "In other words, can you imagine the signal I would have sent had I said, 'Ah, why me? Why am I thrust in the middle of all this stuff?' And they had kids on the front line of combat who were actually having to do all the work."

"You faced some vicious personal attacks," I say.

"I did. But so did Abraham Lincoln." He recalls opening the Abraham Lincoln Presidential Library and Museum in Springfield, Illinois. "There's an exhibit, and the voices of opposition to Lincoln were being played. I said, 'Wow!' This guy, America's—remember now, I got Lincoln's portrait on the wall at the White House and I got a bust of Lincoln—and I hear the people calling him a baboon, just vicious."

When Bush read, in *Presidential Courage*, by Michael Beschloss, that historians were still debating whether George Washington had been a good president, he told Laura that if they were still debating Washington's presidency more than 200 years later, he would not worry what public opinion was saying about him now. "And the other thing for me was that I saw a great man be criticized, as you might recall," he says, referring again to the vitriol aimed at GHWB during the losing reelection campaign of 1992. "On the harshness meter, it seemed unusually harsh to me, as the son. So, therefore, when I became president, the criticism to me was nothing compared to the criticism to him. And so I was able to keep life in perspective two ways: one, through reading of history and how other leaders were treated, but also having witnessed history with my dad."

A book got me back together with President W. after a decade, my own book *The Everlasting Stream*, a memoir of my many years of rabbit hunting with my Kentucky father-in-law and his good-old-boy buddies. In it, I also mentioned my back-and-forth negotiations with GHWB, and my publisher thought it would be great to have a book cover blurb from the former president, who graciously agreed. When the book appeared in the fall of 2002, I sent GHWB a signed copy, along with a signed copy for W. Soon, I got a handwritten note from President W.

"Old #41 gave me your book (which I will soon read)," the president wrote. He gave his best to my family and ended with, "Come by sometime." Then, I got another handwritten letter from the president dated four days later: "I just finished *The Everlasting Stream* and liked it a lot. I told Laura, 'The boy can still write.' . . . Should you ever come back to see what you are missing, check in at the *Post* or rub elbows with the powerful, please call Ashley"—and he gave me his White House secretary's direct dial. "I really enjoy my job . . . " he also wrote. "The only problem with this place is there aren't enough rabbit hunters up here."

I know that two invitations from the president should have spurred me to action, but I wasn't planning to be in Washington until the following August. In the meantime, at the University of Illinois, where I had become a journalism professor after leaving the *Washington Post* in 1996, I was surrounded by students and faculty angry about Bush's impending invasion of Iraq. In my academic cocoon, Bush was called a stupid warmonger trying to avenge his father's failure to oust Saddam Hussein, a stupid warmonger trying to make the world safe for Big Oil, a stupid warmonger trying to prop up his sagging popularity. I told colleagues that I believed Bush—right or wrong—sincerely considered Iraq a deadly threat to the United States, period. My view got me labeled a Bush conservative. Then one morning I got into my academic office building's elevator and saw this scratched into the paint: "Kill Bush."

I had to catch my breath: *Was this America?*

When *New York Times* columnist Maureen Dowd invoked my by-then ancient *Washington Post Magazine* article about GHWB in arguing that W. was little more than "a wealthy white man with the right ancestors," I wrote a column for the *St. Louis Post-Dispatch* responding both to Dowd and to all the vitriol directed toward the president.

"I have told various George W. haters that they had best not underestimate the man," I wrote, "that he's smart, thoughtful in a brawny kind of way and, most of all, a good and decent man. . . . What I've never mentioned is that I didn't vote for George W. I disagree with him on the Supreme Court, environment, abortion, the death penalty and affirmative action. So I voted against this good and decent man. It pained me to do it. . . . It baffles me that grown people must convince themselves that those with whom they disagree are stupid or malevolent."

I didn't hear from the president, but a few days later, I got a poignant letter from his father. "Tell those kids in your class not to give up on POTUS," he wrote, using the popular acronym for president of the United States. "Tell them life for a president is not easy, yet I have never heard #43 whine about the loneliest job on earth, never seen him pose gazing out into the future to depict how tough his job is. Walt, he does not want war. He does want Iraq to do what it has pledged to do. Have you ever seen a president face so many tough problems all at once? I haven't." The elder Bush was clearly feeling as much pain over the criticism of his son as W. had felt over the criticism of his father.

I figured that after publicly declaring that I had not voted for W., the invitations to the White House would cease. Yet when I was in Washington the following August, in 2003—three months after the "Mission Accomplished" speech aboard the USS *Abraham Lincoln*—I called Ashley, as directed. To my astonishment, Ashley called back and said the president would love to see me. In the early evening a couple days later, I pulled into the southeast gate to the White House.

"Where should I park?" I asked the officer.

"Anywhere in the lot," he said. "Who are you here to see?"

"President Bush."

"Oh," he sputtered, "then pull up along the circle and park at the White House."

I rolled my little '95 Toyota Camry up to the back door, where mine was the only car. A polite Secret Service agent met me, and up I went again in the White House elevator. When the doors opened, there was President W., wearing, as I recall, a rather garish flower-print shirt and casual cream-colored slacks.

"Walt, how are you?" I remember him asking as he hugged me with one arm.

"I'm well, Mr. President. And you?"

The president had two cigars in the other hand, and he offered me one. "You still smoke cigars?" he asked.

"I thought you had gotten rid of all your bad habits," I said, as we walked through the long, elegant center hall in the second-floor residence.

"I still curse a little bit, too," he said, laughing. "Let's go out on the balcony," meaning the Truman Balcony, which overlooks the South Lawn and the Washington Monument.

The president gestured for me to sit facing the beautiful, sunny vista, and he sat facing me, his back to the yard. We lit up, puffed on our cigars, caught up on family news, talked briefly about my memoir and my column in the *Post-Dispatch*, which he had read. I could think of only one question to ask him: "What is it like to be president of the United States?"

President Bush leaned forward, put his elbows on his knees, and stared at me intently. "Are we off the record?"

"Yes."

And he began to talk—and talk and talk for what must have been nearly three hours. I've never told anyone the specifics of what he said that night, not even my wife or closest friends. I did not make notes later and have only my memory. In the journalism world, off the record is off the record. But I have repeatedly described the hours as "amazing," "remarkable," "stunning."

President Bush—and he was, no doubt, by then a real president— talked expansively about Afghanistan, Iraq, Iran, China, Korea, Russia. He talked about his reelection strategies, Iran's nuclear ambitions, WMD and how he still believed they would be found, Colin Powell and Condoleezza Rice, Vladimir Putin. He talked about his aides and how tough their lives were, the long hours and stress and time away from their families, about how difficult it was for his daughters. He said that compared with everyone around a president, the president had the easiest job. He was the same confident, brash man I had met years ago, but I no longer sensed any hint of the old anger or the need for self-aggrandizement.

As he talked, I even thought about an old *Saturday Night Live* skit in which an amiable, bumbling President Ronald Reagan, played by Phil Hartman, goes behind closed doors to suddenly become a masterful operator in total charge at the White House. The transformation in Bush was that stunning to me. Perhaps a half-hour into the conversation, we were joined by Bush's campaign media adviser, Mark McKinnon, whom Bush had nicknamed "M-Kat."

"M-Kat used to be a Democrat, too," Bush quipped, referring to me. "I converted him."

After about an hour, Bush said that Laura was out of town and asked if McKinnon and I would like to join him for dinner. We did, of course, and we moved into the residence dining room, where Bush sat at the head of the table, McKinnon and I on either side, while the president's black cat, Willie, lounged on the far end. Really, he just kept talking. I thought perhaps it was my naiveté that was making the evening seem so remarkable. But when the president was called away from the table for a few minutes, I asked McKinnon if working in the White House was as demanding as Bush had said. He said it was, and then he got a sort of faraway look in his eyes. "But then you have an evening like tonight," I remember him saying. I left the White House in a daze. I even got lost in the pitch-black darkness and had to drive around the small parking lot for a few minutes to find my way to the gate. I called my wife, and she asked how the evening had gone. I couldn't answer.

"I've never known you to be speechless," she said, genuinely surprised.

I finally said, "It was like sitting and listening to Michael Jordan talk basketball or Pavarotti talk opera, listening to someone at the top of his game share his secrets."

My takeaway: *what a difference a decade had made.*

In the remaining years of his presidency, I visited Bush several more times, always in the Oval Office. He was candid, but nothing like that first night. His only remark about Barack Obama was, as I recall it, "No matter who wins, when he hears what I hear every morning, it will change him." When I met with Bush in the summer of 2008, after eating hot dogs alone together in the little dining room off the Oval Office, he put his hand on my shoulder and said he wanted me to help him with his memoir. In my spit-and-vinegar youth, I would never have considered using my journalism skills in service to a politician. But the idea of eavesdropping on the private stories of one of only 43 men who had ever held the presidency was too compelling. I told him I would help. A couple months later, I got a handwritten note from the president thanking me for my willingness but saying he had decided "to go a different route."

I was not surprised. The president is a tough grader. I must have scored only a B+.

President Bush has just about lipped his cigar to death, but still he keeps working it. "The job of the president is to be strategic in thought and to look over the horizon," he says, waving the soggy cigar. "And history helps a president look over the horizon." In the White House, Bush sometimes read for pleasure in the Treaty Room, the president's private office, lounging back in its comfortable chair with his feet up on the desk, or while exercising on the elliptical machine. But mostly, he read, as he had in Midland, at night in bed. "Reading books," Bush says, "means you're not lonely."

In *Decision Points*, Bush cites book after book that influenced his thinking in the White House. The Bible, for one, and he quotes Lincoln, who called it "the best gift God has given to man." After 9/11, he thought of Lincoln's declaration that the battle between freedom and tyranny was "an issue which can only be tried by war, and decided by victory"—words, he says, that framed his policy toward the war on terror. He cites *Supreme Command* by Eliot Cohen, a strategic studies professor at Johns Hopkins University, who argued that a president must hold his generals accountable for results. And *Dereliction of Duty* by Colonel H. R. McMaster, who argued that the Vietnam War military leadership had not done enough to correct the flawed strategy adopted by President Johnson and Defense Secretary Robert McNamara. In Iraq, the counterinsurgency strategy of "clear, hold, and build" employed by McMaster, who had become commander of the 3rd Armored Cavalry regiment, replaced the failed strategy of "train-and-withdraw" used by Bush's generals at the start of the war.

Just after his 2004 reelection, Bush read *The Case for Democracy* by Natan Sharansky, a Soviet dissident who had spent nine years in the gulag and who reported that he and his fellow political prisoners had been inspired by then-President Ronald Reagan's clarion—some said belligerent—call for freedom in the Soviet empire. Bush decided that he, too, would be clear in that call. In his Second Inaugural, he intoned: "So it is the policy of the United States to seek and support the growth of democratic movements and institutions in every nation and culture, with the ultimate goal of ending tyranny in our world."

Bush also emphasizes that he made decisions as president so as not to repeat what history had convinced him were the mistakes of former presidents. He relented on changes in his controversial Terrorist Surveillance Program when his acting attorney general, James Comey, and FBI Director Robert Mueller threatened to resign over aspects of it. He didn't want a repeat of President Richard M. Nixon's infamous Saturday Night Massacre, when Nixon's attorney general and deputy attorney general resigned after refusing to fire Watergate prosecutor Archibald Cox. Bush also was determined not to micromanage the military planning in Afghanistan and Iraq, as he believed Johnson and McNamara had done in Vietnam. Although his critics would disagree, he also believes he took care not to repeat the wartime overreactions that had led to the Alien and Sedition Acts of 1798 under John Adams, Lincoln's suspension of habeas corpus, or Roosevelt's internment of Japanese Americans during World War II.

I ask what he believes is the most important quality in great leaders.

"Willingness to stand on principle, the notion that public opinion changes back and forth and that you shouldn't chase public opinion. . . . Lincoln had a set of principles that were important to him. 'All men are created equal under God' is the ultimate. It's the ultimate principle for America's freedom. . . . But Lincoln acted on it in a difficult political environment. People forget that he was in a very tough reelection campaign, and it wasn't until Sherman makes it to Atlanta that his prospects brightened. Secondly, Lincoln had a strategic vision for the country. One of the great presidential decisions ever was to keep the country intact. . . . The question oftentimes in history is what would have happened if a different decision were made. We'd have been Europe."

Of his own presidency, he says, "Obviously, there were some very difficult moments, and there was some doubt as to whether or not decisions I had made were going to become fruitful. But I also realized there's a whole history of what would have happened, what are the consequences had you not made a decision. So, like on Saddam Hussein, maybe it's a historian's perspective . . . but no doubt in my mind, if he were in power today, all that's happening in the Middle East now would be much more dangerous." And what might have happened in Libya during the recent uprising, Bush asks, if he and British Prime Minister Tony Blair hadn't convinced Qaddafi to give up his weapons of mass destruction? The same logic applied, he says, during the financial meltdown during his last months in office. Ben Bernanke, the Federal Reserve chairman and a preeminent historian on the causes of the Great Depression, told Bush that unless he did something drastic, the nation would descend into depression.

"Well, I had read enough history about the Depression to know the consequences. . . . I didn't want history to record that there was a moment when George W. Bush could have done something to prevent the depression and chose not to." We don't know if inaction would have resulted in a depression, he says—only that he did act and there was no depression. "It's just one of those moments where you just had to move one way or the other. And I moved."

I ask, "What did you see as your principles?"

"One of them was 'freedom is universal,' which was unbelievably controversial for a period of time during my presidency, which, frankly, astonished me, given my reading of history." He paraphrases his Second Inaugural: "We'll resist tyranny at all times, all places, basically. Well, to me, you could say that was inspired by Lincoln. . . . Based upon the principle that deep in everybody's soul is the desire to be free. And what's interesting is, it's playing out right now," he says, referring to the populist uprisings in the Middle East.

"The interesting thing about Egypt was that of all the countries in the Middle East, Egypt had a great chance to become an example of democracy. And President Mubarak, after '82, chose not to head that way. Eventually, though, the young, educated, unemployed said, 'Wait a minute! We're tired of it!' I wasn't surprised. I wasn't surprised when the people of Iraq went to vote. I really wasn't. And took enormous risks to vote. Or the people in Afghanistan. Unbelievably inspirational moments as far as I was concerned. Others didn't see it that way, I fully understood. But, to me, it was validation of the concept that all want to be free."

His decision to launch the military surge in Iraq in 2007, at a time when the military situation was deteriorating and American public opinion had turned overwhelmingly against the war, was rooted in what he saw as the central principle of his presidency and the question historians would ask about what would happen if he did not make the decision. "The surge was, one, a belief that freedom is universal and, therefore, if given a chance, people will seize the moment. And the other calculation was, 'What does failure mean?'"

So how will history judge his presidency?

"Some people walk up and say, 'Oh, man, history is going to judge you well.' And my quip is, 'I'm not going to be around to see it.' And to me, that's one of the most important lessons you learn through history—you're just not gonna be around to see it. . . . I'm confident of this: that those conclusions will be more objective with time than they could conceivably be now."

I ask if he thinks President Obama has read his book.

He laughs. "If somebody said he hasn't had time to read it yet, I'd say, 'I understand.'"

I visited President Bush in the Oval Office one more time. I was thinking about doing a book about how Americans pray, and I had remembered that way back in Midland, he had advised me to read the Bible cover-to-cover, something I had done since then. He agreed to talk with me about his prayer life, and, for a final time, I journeyed to the Oval Office.

"I've thought about this conversation a lot since you asked . . . " President Bush said. "I'm learning and have been learning ever since 1986, really."

That afternoon, only a few months before he would leave office, we sat beneath the famous Rembrandt Peale portrait of George Washington, and President Bush told me that he prayed daily in the White House. He prayed for spiritual insight—to "be more discerning of the Word of God." He prayed that God keep his wife and daughters protected. He prayed that our soldiers and their families be given comfort and strength. He did not pray for good weather on his daughter's wedding day, or that his father's hip surgery go well, or that the stock market rise.

"Do you pray, 'Dear God, let Congress get it right?' " I asked.

"No."

" 'Dear God, let Pelosi get it right?' "

"No, no, no, no, no, God is not the minority leader"—and then he laughed and corrected himself. "Majority leader. . . . Nor do I pray for a Republican victory. . . . I really don't."

He prayed before his presidential debates, kept a little cross in his pocket that he would squeeze: " 'Dear God, I pray that I speak clearly and bring calm.' " He prayed before his State of the Union addresses, alone in the little holding room: " 'Dear God, I pray that you shine through me today.' "

"And the prayers of the people," he said, referring to those who pray for him, "this is where I get into a little shaky ground because I can't prove it." But Bush said he had actually felt the prayers of people asking God to comfort him. "And so the pop psychologists say, 'Well, he's grasping for affection.' . . . I tell people all the time this—that the prayers of the people matter. And I do have a sense of calm." Perhaps, he said, his prayers and the prayers of others are the reason. "I've been asked this some: 'Do you think God wanted you to go to war?' I didn't ask in prayer. . . . I don't think that's fair to God to do that."

"Have you prayed, 'Dear God, if I was wrong about this, forgive me?' "

"No, no, no. First of all, I don't believe I'm wrong about it. I don't believe it's wrong to confront evil. And I don't believe it's wrong to give people the opportunity to live in a free society. . . . I don't want to bring God down into a presidential debate over 'yes' or 'no' into Iraq."

"Do you have compassion for your enemy?"

"I have yet to forgive Osama bin Laden, and, frankly, haven't prayed [for him] because I think he needs to be brought to justice in order to prevent him from killing other people."

"Isn't it possible to pray for Osama bin Laden and also want to bring him to justice?"

"I'm not sophisticated enough in prayer, evidently, to be able to pray for Osama bin Laden and at the same time go hunt him."

Early the next morning, my hotel phone rang me out of bed.

"The president would like to talk with you," a pleasant voice said.

In a moment, President Bush was on the line. He said he didn't want to leave me with a wrong impression: he did pray regularly for forgiveness. He just wanted to be sure I knew that.

I thanked him for the call.

"Well," he said with a laugh, "now you can tell your friends that the president of the United States gave you a wake-up call."

# MY FATHER, MY SON, MY SELF

What do fathers and sons see in each other?
Themselves.

**M**y father's guitar has his name, Len, printed immodestly in three-inch iridescent letters on its body, and they glisten as he tunes up to play for my son. His lyrics, scrawled into homemade booklets, are spread out on the floor, the kitchen sink, the music stand. As ever, my father takes his hootenannies seriously. He has always had this goose-like way of craning his neck as he reads. And silhouetted against a single lamp, he does this as he peers through silver reading glasses that are oddly oversized for his head. Knowing what a skinflint my father is, I figure he got a deal on them a long time ago and they've been falling off into his soup ever since. At 67, my dad still looks as I remember him, hair full and brown, body trim, face tanned, eyes sharp. What's different, what I can't get used to, is his gentleness and his patience. I remember neither as a boy, and I wonder which of us has changed. My son is 4, and as my dad thumbs through his children's songs, Matthew bounces on the couch, furtively strums the guitar he's not supposed to touch and talks incessantly.

"You know 'Give Me a Home Where the Buffalo Roam'?" my father asks in the high-pitched, teasing voice he reserves for kids and, on occasion, my mother.

"No," says Matthew. "We gotta find some I know, right, Grandpa?"

"Yep."

"Right!"

"How 'bout 'I Been Workin' on the Railroad'?"

"Yeah! I know that one. You know why? One time I heard my daddy sing it. So I know it too." Then with a fierce pride that shoots through me unexpectedly, Matthew adds, "My daddy taught it to me!"

I think to myself: And so it begins.

How I once despised that benign old man. I don't recall why I despised him, only that I did. And that I made sure he knew it. All the classic stuff, the painful yet gleeful realization that he didn't know everything, the shouting matches, the weird friends and clothes and beliefs—it all seems surreal today. But I still recall vividly my two great revelations about my dad. The first came sometime in my late teens when I suddenly realized that I was not my father, and that I could stop trying to prove that I wasn't. The second came about age 30 when I realized, in contradiction to my first revelation, that I was my father, like it or not. By then, I'd come to like it. What this says about my Freudian profile, who knows? These things came down between my father and me, and that is that.

There's so much talk these days about the New Fatherhood. Freed from being the sole paycheck, fathers no longer carry the pride or the burden of being the family giant-killer who goes off to battle the world every day. They baby-sit, wash laundry, mix formula. And fathers today are able to do what fathers of the last generation couldn't do for their sons: They hug them and kiss them and tell them they love them. These changes have liberated fathers from an isolation they once suffered within their own families.

Even knowing these things, a friend of mine once lamented the passing of the old bonds between father and son—the hunting trips, the tinkering with the old jalopy, the undisputed authority of Father, the unrelenting masculinity of his model. "What's left for a father to teach his son?" my friend asked.

I've thought about that a lot lately, which is predictable after having had a son, and I now see my father with what seems a remarkable clarity. And instead of finding my father in myself, I now find myself in my father. I don't have my father's voice; we share a voice. I don't have my father's humor; we share a humor. I don't have my father's stubbornness; we share a stubbornness. I didn't always see these similarities as desirable. But I've grown into them. My father, for instance, has this way of answering the phone. "Hellll-o," he says, putting a heavy accent on the first syllable and snapping the o short. I picked this up as a boy and dropped it along the way. But call me today and you'll hear, "Hellll-o," just like the old man. Every time I hear myself say it, I feel good. I've grown into it.

On the way to the hardware store recently, my boy asked, "Sons can grow up to be their daddies, right, Dad?" This was no small struggling for insight, and I was careful in my response. No, I said, sons can't grow up to be their daddies. They can grow up to do the same work or to be like their daddies in some ways, but they can't be their daddies. They must be themselves. My son would hear nothing of these subtleties. He insisted that his friend Justin would grow up to be his daddy and that he would grow up to be me.

"Sons can grow up to be their daddies!" he said defiantly. "They can."

I didn't argue. It made me feel good.


My dad wasn't around much when I was a boy. He worked seven days a week and built our house in his spare time. But I've got plenty of warm memories—my father and me on the couch watching TV, riding the tractor, walking the gravel road at dusk, riding home at night in a darkened car singing "Red River Valley." Wedges of time between miles of distance.

He was a good man, my father, and I knew it then. He laughed easily and was the life of a party, playing the guitar, singing, organizing the games. He also was a rugged teaser, and it was during his teasing that I always sensed his great, unspoken love. When I was older I would learn that this is how men show affection without acknowledging vulnerability. I'm sure there was a time when I yearned to be with my father more. But the day came very early when I also dreaded his presence. He was stern, with a quick temper. Even when at work he was the taskmaster in absentia. Infractions were added up, and at night my father dispensed punishment. This rarely went beyond a threatening voice and a scolding finger, and never beyond spanking, but in time my father's masculine warmth paled next to his feared judgment. When he was around, life seemed harder. I was in trouble more, there was less laughter and silliness, more attention to correct behavior. It was as if my father was trying to cram a lifetime of teaching into the little time we had together.

But there are things a boy cannot understand. I didn't understand, for instance, that my parents were a short step from poor. I didn't understand that my father had worked in the steel mill for 85 cents an hour before I was born and that he was fired when he refused to work nights, refused to leave my mother and my sister at home alone. I didn't understand that we lived from paycheck to paycheck and that he got up at 3:30 every morning to deliver milk because he had no choice. I just knew that he was a stranger in our house. He appeared occasionally, announced decisions, passed judgment. It was the way fatherhood went in those days. And like so many others of that era, my sisters, mother and I fell into a pact to maneuver around the slumbering bear. "That's your father," my mother would say with pleasant resignation.

When he was home, my father was the boss, no question. But when he was gone, which was most of the time, rules were less stringent, conversation and feelings more free. My mother became the emotional fulcrum. It seemed that I could tell her anything, while I could tell him nothing. At least nothing that counted, nothing of the heart or the soul. If I was angry at my father, I told my mother, knowing she'd pass it on. If my father was sorry he'd yelled at me, my mother would relay his apology. "Dad didn't mean it," she'd say. "He's just tired tonight." None of this seemed weird. And not until I was a father myself did I discover that my father wasn't only the perpetrator, but also the victim, of this little dynamic.

But I never doubted my father's love, which was our lifeline through some pretty rough times. Always, he had this way of smiling at me, this way of tossing a backhanded compliment that let me know he was proud and watchful of my achievements. He was no insecure bully. I teased him plenty. And I imitated his way of saying "I love you" by telling him his nose was too big or his ties too ugly.

But even today I can't recall a time my father hugged me or kissed me or said he loved me. I remember sleeping next to him on Sunday mornings. I remember the strong, warm feeling of him holding me as I dozed off in his arms. But men, even little men, did not kiss or hug, they shook hands. There were times much later, times when I would be going back to college, with the car packed and my parents and me standing on the driveway in those final few seconds, times when I wanted so badly to hug my father. But the muscles wouldn't move with the emotion. I hugged my mother. My dad and I shook hands.

"It's not what a man says, but what he does that counts," my father would say. Words and emotions were suspect. He went to work every day, he protected me, he taught me right from wrong, he made me tough in mind and spirit.

It was our bond. It was our barrier.

Matthew and I, visiting my parents in Arizona, are out for a walk. We see my folks rarely, and the chance to spend an entire week with his grandfather is a treat for my son, who seems especially bent right now on comprehending his place in time and family and gender. We leave the grandparents back at their winter trailer to rest from Matthew's frenetic energy.

"When I'm grown up," Matthew says, "I'll be walking here with my boy, right? You'll be back at the trailer with Mommy, right? You'll be old."

No matter how often I hear my son make these kinds of connections, I am amazed. They seem to blare from a loudspeaker, making me stop and turn my head in an involuntary pause. It's as if history is breaking before my eyes. Yes, that's right, I tell him, you will be walking here with your son, and your mother and I will be back at the trailer and Grandma and Grandpa will be dead. I wait for his reaction. There is none.

Matthew is at a nice age for fathers. It's all glory. A neighbor, who is 6 feet 5, recalls that when his son was about Matthew's age, the boy believed he had the tallest dad in the world. My neighbor was deeply saddened when his boy met a man who was taller. It just can't last. Here is how another friend describes his son's transformation from adoring boy to resentful teen: "When he was 6, he'd ask me a question and I'd answer it. He'd say, 'Dad knows everything!' When he was 14, I'd answer a question and he'd say, 'Dad thinks he knows everything!' It could have been the same question."

Like so many so-called New Fathers, I've tried not to repeat what I saw as my father's mistakes. I've refused to be the enforcer, expecting my wife to take an equal role, because I know what that did to my father and me. Matthew and I talk about emotions. We touch and cuddle and kiss goodbye. I try never to be embarrassed about this, though I suspect he senses my occasional uneasiness. This is the new masculinity, and it's as common today as the old masculinity was in my father's day. But, honestly, I'm not one who believes this will in the end save Matthew and me from what novelist Larry L. King calls the "mutual thirst to prevail" between father and son. All I hope is that we build some repository of unconscious joy so that it will remain a lifeline between us through some pretty rough times. Because being a father simply isn't that new.

I remember once coming home from college and sitting at the dinner table lecturing my father about something. On and on I went. Now, my father loves a good argument, but as I talked that night he ate passively, occasionally glancing up, giving me that smile. Finally, I asked insistently, "Well, what do you think?" Without interrupting the arch of his fork from plate to mouth, my father looked into my eyes and said slowly and quietly, "Yep, you're still the same old knucklehead." I can't tell you how many times I've laughed at that memory because some things really never do change.

If there is a universal complaint from men about their fathers, it's that their dads lacked patience. I've thought of my own father's impatience a great deal in the last few years: as I painted my house and Matthew insisted he help, as I remodeled my second floor and Matthew insisted he help, as I sawed down dead trees in the backyard and Matthew insisted he help. At these times, and plenty more, memories of my father's impatience came clearly to mind. Because no matter the task, I never seemed to get it done right or get it done fast enough for him. It seemed that as soon as I'd started, my father would intervene: "Here, let me finish that up for you." God, I hated that.

So am I better with my own son? Well, I always start out with that in mind. I feign patience, give him a brush or a hammer, play along for a while. But in the end, I explain that these chores must be done, that they are dangerous and that he'll have to find something else to do because I can't work and watch out for him at the same time. I sometimes say this patiently, sometimes less so, considerably less so. But no matter how I say it, there's a scene. And I suspect that one of these encounters will live engraved on my son's mind as the lifelong example of the old man's ill temper.

At least it was that way for me. I remember a lousy, dark and rainy day when I was about 6 and my father was putting a new roof on his mother's house. I, of course, wanted to help. When my father said no, I made a scene and got the only spanking that I can recall. My father has chuckled at that memory many times over the years, but I never really saw the humor. It had happened decades earlier, but I still saw it through the eyes of a 6-year-old boy. Only now that I've struggled to find patience in myself with my own son am I able to see that day through my father's eyes. I mean, climbing around on a roof is dangerous enough when it's dry, much less wet. Besides, the man had the shingles torn off and the rain was pouring into my grandmother's house. He was cold and wet and, to use a modern term, under stress. You see, I've put a new roof on in the pouring rain since that day. It's a miserable job—and the concerns of a little boy look mighty insubstantial in comparison. Who'd have guessed I'd be angry about that day for 30 years, until I could relive it with my own son, who, I suppose, is angry at me about it now.

But this empathy for my father finally led me to a startling insight: If I am still resolving my feelings about my father, then when I was a boy my father was still resolving his feelings about his father. He raised me as a result of and a reaction to his own dad, which links my son not only to me and my father, but to my father's father and, I suspect, any number of Harrington fathers before. That realized, I suddenly imagined that if the phone had rung as the first Harrington stepped off the boat, he'd have answered by saying, "Hellll-o."

When I am with my father and my son, it is sometimes as if I don't exist, as if I am only a bridge separating and uniting these two people. For instance, I have this way of negotiating with Matthew about daily matters. "Do we have a deal?" I ask. "Yeah," he responds, "we have a deal." Then one day, I seem to disappear when I hear my father ask Matthew, "Well, do we have a deal?" These reprises go on constantly, most of them more subtle than words.

I am, for example, proud of my son's curiosity, a quality I've always liked in myself. But as my father and Matthew and I drive back to Arizona from California, where we had visited my sister, it is again as if I've disappeared.

"Wanta stop?" my father asks enthusiastically as we pass someplace called Bible Land, where an old sculptor has spent his entire life crafting sandstone Bible scenes in an open field. Nobody says yes, but my dad's driving, so we stop. In California's rich Imperial Valley we hear all about gravity irrigation systems and stop to see Old King Solomon, the first date tree imported to California. I ask how long it takes an orange grove to bear fruit after planting. "I don't know," my dad says. "I'll have to find that out." We learn the names of countless cacti and grasses, that hornets don't fly at night, which is nice to know, and that ants don't eat fish. We learn the price of gasoline at every station we pass. We stop in the desert to admire the dunes.

"Look over there," my father says suddenly, pointing to an endless horizon of sand. "Look at that lonesome mountain back there." There's a silence until he says, "Everything's beautiful if you just look at it right."

I disappear. It is a sentence I have said to my own son.

There is a time in every son's life when he is angered by the echoes reminding him that, for all his vaunted individuality, he is his father's son. But there should also come a time when these echoes call out only a profound repose, neither nostalgic nor exhilarating, and the understanding that the generations have melded and blurred without threat. I am not my father. We still disagree on just about everything to do with politics and society, and, plagued with more education, I'm far less confident that the world as I see it is necessarily as it is. I can't bait a fish hook, repair an engine or stalk a pheasant. John Wayne is not my idol.

Yet these matters aren't of consequence. And looking back, I sometimes think my father's generation was right: "It's not what a man says, but what he does that counts." Because if I ever learned anything from my dad's lectures, I don't recall it. I hold him responsible and I love him not for what he said, but for what he did or didn't do. Because what good fathers have always taught their sons, more or less unconsciously, isn't a checklist of hunting and fishing skills, but what it means to be a man, some seedling sense of how to be strong but not destructive, self-reliant but not invulnerable, of what self-mastery means in a world we must pretend to control when we can't.

I once believed that manhood required that I stand up to my father, even if it meant fists. And then this happened: Some friends and I buried our high school's parking-lot barriers under the woodpile for the annual Homecoming bonfire. We hated the things because they kept us from leaving school in our cars until after the buses had left. I thought the prank was pretty funny and I mentioned it to my dad. He didn't think it was funny and he ordered me to go with him to dig them out of the pile. Can you imagine anything more humiliating at age 16? I refused, and we stood toe to toe. My father was in a rage, and I thought for an instant that the test had come. But then he shook his head and calmly walked away. The next day, my friends told me they'd seen him at the bonfire celebration that night, that he'd climbed into the woodpile before hundreds of kids, pulled out the barriers and left. He never mentioned it to me. He still hasn't.

For reasons too profound and too petty to tell, there was a time years ago when my father and I didn't speak or see each other. I finally gave up my stubbornness and visited unexpectedly. For two days we talked of cars and work, politics and old friends, of everything and nothing. Neither mentioned that we hadn't seen each other in five years. During a Sunday snowstorm, I left as depressed as I've ever been, knowing that reconciliation was impossible. Two days later I got the only letter my dad ever sent me. I'm the writer, he's the milkman? Ha! The letter's tone and cadence, its emotion and simplicity might have been mine.

"I know that if I had it to do over again," my father wrote, "I would somehow find more time to spend with you. It seems we never realize this until it's too late." It turned out that as he had watched me walk out that door—at the very instant I was thinking that we were hopelessly lost to each other—he was telling himself to stop me, to sit down and talk, that if we didn't, he would never see me again. "But I just let you go," he wrote. The muscles wouldn't move with the emotion, which is all I ever really needed to know.

All morning I am anxious. Matthew and I leave Arizona today for home and I am determined to do something I have never done. I am determined to tell my father that I love him. I fret over the timing, knowing that there will be little left to say after that unheard-of declaration. Not surprisingly, I opt for the easy route, the last minute before Matthew and I walk through the gate and onto the plane.

"Dad, I want you to know that I love you. That I always have."

There is a bag in my left hand and I lean over and hug my father with my right arm. He is impassive. I suppose he's in shock.

"Yeah, yeah sure," he says awkwardly. "No problem."

And then we are gone. It wouldn't surprise me if my father turned to my mother, shook his head, and said, "Yep, he's still the same old knucklehead." But now, after my own voyage, it also wouldn't surprise me if he cried. Knowing that, I hope, will someday make it easier for me, and for my son.

# PERMISSIONS

# ABOUT THE AUTHOR

Walt Harrington is a former staff writer for the *Washington Post Magazine*, where he wrote benchmark profiles of Jesse Jackson, Jerry Falwell, Bryan Stevenson, Rosa Parks and George H. W. Bush, as well as numerous in-depth stories on the lives of ordinary people. He is the author or editor of ten books, an Emmy-winning documentary film writer, and a Professor Emeritus at the University of Illinois, where he taught literary journalism and served as head of the Department of Journalism and as an associate chancellor.

# ABOUT THE PUBLISHERS

NeoText is a publisher of quality fiction and long-form journalism. Visit the NeoText website at NeoTextCorp.com

The Sager Group was founded in 1984. In 2012 it was chartered as a multimedia content brand, with the intent of empowering those who create art—an umbrella beneath which makers can pursue, and profit from, their craft directly, without gatekeepers. TSG publishes books; ministers to artists and provides modest grants; and produces documentary, feature, and commercial films. By harnessing the means of production, The Sager Group helps artists help themselves. For more information, please see TheSagerGroup.net.

# ABOUT THE STACKS READER SERIES

The Stacks Reader Series highlights classic literary non-fiction and short fiction by great journalists that would otherwise be lost to history—a living archive of memorable storytelling by notable authors. Curated by Alex Belth and brought to you by The Sager Group.

Artifex Te Adiuva